W9-BNM-778

"For more than four decades, Jenny Pruitt has led with a servant's heart in the Atlanta realty arena. In this account of her life story, Beneath His Wings, Jenny suggests that the leadership principles she follows—acknowledgment of God's role first, character, commitment, generosity, leading by loving, and continuing to learn and grow—will also lead to living a successful life."

— John C. Maxwell
Author, Speaker, Leadership Expert

"Jenny Pruitt is a fierce competitor whose success is grounded in her faith and her determination. The fact that all proceeds of this book will go to charitable organizations that glorify God is a testimony to both."

— Senator Johnny Isakson
U. S. Senator from Georgia

"Beneath His Wings is the most practical compass for aligning professional and spiritual goals that I have seen. Jenny's heartfelt story is one of faith and triumph—a must-read for anyone longing for inspiration and guidance."

— Carol B. Tome
CFO, Executive V. P., Corporate
The Home Depot

"In her autobiography, Jenny Pruitt offers an insightful, inspiring story of courage and deep faith. Her openness and candor provide encouragement, not only in handling success with good grace and authenticity, but also in overcoming life's inevitable setbacks and disappointments. Beneath His Wings offers compelling evidence of the fact that professional success and religious faith are not mutually exclusive.

— Frank Skinner
Former CEO and Chairman
BellSouth Telecommunications

"She may have it all in the eyes of the world—having attained success in the competitive field of real estate and having garnered many awards and accolades as a businesswoman and philanthropist. But as Jenny Pruitt's captivating book Beneath His Wings reveals, her highest calling and desire is to be a servant of Jesus Christ. We highly recommend this beautiful account of her remarkable life!"

— Debbie and Michael W. Smith
Singer/Songwriter

"Jenny Pruitt tells a story that many women can relate to—juggling the responsibilities of family and career. Jenny's journey, like all of us, has its ups and downs; but through it all, she confesses that the secret to life is learning to walk with the Lord Jesus Christ every step of the way. Finding comfort in His forgiveness and love, she looks back over the decades with great joy in living life beneath His wings."

— Franklin Graham
President and CEO
Billy Graham Evangelistic Association
Samaritan's Purse

"In today's world, it is rare to find a highly successful businessman or woman who is willing to be completely transparent. In her autobiography, Beneath His Wings, Jenny Pruitt is not only transparent—readers can see all the way to her heart of gold. This book, promoting not herself but God, may be Jenny's finest legacy."

— Andy Stanley
Founding Pastor
North Point Ministries

"Jenny Pruitt and I share a mutual love for Atlanta, homes, and the families who live there. Jenny is a powerful inspirational servant leader. In this honest reveal of a remarkable life, she demonstrates how the nearly overwhelming obstacles she has faced in business and in her personal life have only brought her closer to God. Jenny's story will teach, inspire, and cause readers to understand that the challenges they face can make them stronger and more effective if they stay nestled close to Him."

— Ann Platz
Designer, Author, Speaker

"At this dark and critical time in history, Jenny Pruitt's story has what our country needs: (1) desperate departure from self-reliance; (2) a journey of faith that is authentic and transparent; (3) tips for succeeding in all walks of life; and (4) most importantly, giving God all the glory! In a skeptical and cynical world, Jenny's life story proves that His ways are better than ours."

— Mickey Robinson
International Speaker, Author
Prophetic Destiny International

Beneath His Wings

Beneath His Wings

JENNY PRUITT

WITH ANNE SEVERANCE

FOREWORD BY CHARLES STANLEY

BENEATH HIS WINGS
Copyright © 2015 by Jenny Pruitt
Published in Partnership with:
BelieversPress
5585 Erindale Drive, #200 Colorado Springs, CO 80918

All rights reserved. No part of this publication may be reproduced, stored in a retrieval system, or transmitted in any form or by any means- electronic, mechanical, photocopying, recording, or otherwise— without the prior written permission of the publisher.

Unless otherwise indicated, all Scripture quotations are taken from the Holy Bible, New Living Translation, copyright © 1996, 2004. Used by permission of Tyndale House Publishers, Inc., Wheaton, Illinois 60189. All rights reserved.

Scripture quotations marked NKJV **are taken from** *The New King James Version.* **Copyright © 1979, 1980, 1982, Thomas Nelson, Inc.**

Scripture quotations marked NIV **are taken** from *The Holy Bible: New International Version®* NIV ®. © 1973, 1978, 1984 by International Bible Society. Used by permission of Zondervan Publishing House. All rights reserved.

Scripture quotations marked NCV are taken from the *New Century Version®,* copyright © 2005 by Thomas Nelson. Used by permission.

Scripture quotations marked TLB are taken from *The Living Bible* copyright © 1971. Used by permission of Tyndale House Publishers, Inc., Wheaton, Illinois 60189. All rights reserved.

Cover photography and design: Jamey Guy
Hair styled by Danielle Turner
Interior design: Samizdat Creative

Library of Congress Cataloging-in-Publication Data
Hardcover: 978-0-578-16563-9
Softcover: 978-0-578-16564-6
ePUB: 978-0-578-16565-3
MOBI: 978-0-578-16701-5

Library of Congress Control Number: 2015913384

Printed by: Bethany Press
Printed in the United States of America

Contents

To Bob, the love of my life
and the wind beneath my wings

To my angel daughters, Stephanie and Susan

To my business partner and son-in-law,
David Boehmig

and

To my seven grand-angels:
Sarah, Ben, Abigail, Jack, Matthew, Emily, and Zach

Foreword

*A*S HER PASTOR FOR over sixteen years, I have known Jenny Pruitt as a godly woman, fine artist, and talented businesswoman. She has always given her best in love and service to Jesus. So you can imagine my delight when I received her book, *Beneath His Wings*.

This book is Jenny's testimony of how she has interacted with God through the mountains and valleys of life and depended on Him every step of the way. Jenny shares her inspiring journey of faith through the death of her father, relational difficulties, cancer, and the struggles and challenges of owning a business. With prayer, reliance on God's Word, and a transparent heart, Jenny relates how the Father walked with her through all the storms she has faced and taught her the most important lessons of her life.

Despite these difficulties, Jenny has always embraced God's will—no matter the cost to her personally. She listens when He speaks. She follows His lead, then encourages others to do the same. In fact, Jenny loves to mentor, to help other people become all they were meant to be. She never misses an opportunity to point them to the One who has sheltered her and brought her through.

I'm proud of Jenny—the woman of faith she has become, her excellent testimony and ministry. In fact, she was sitting in my office one day many years ago, having already become successful in the real estate field, when she told me she felt God might be calling her to foreign missions. Her husband, on the other hand, didn't feel the same call.

"Look around you, Jenny," I said to her that day. "Look at all the hurting people. Your ministry is the marketplace." She took up that challenge, and this book is the rest of the story.

Truly, Jenny has found freedom and victory beneath the Father's wings, and you can, too. I am confident you will be both inspired and encouraged as you read her life story and learn the godly principles that paved the way to her success—to the glory of God.

CHARLES STANLEY
Senior Pastor, First Baptist, Atlanta
Founder and President, In Touch Ministries
June 2015

Introduction

*R*ECENTLY, A NEW WORLD opened before me—dazzling in its promise. Having worked as a businesswoman most of my life, I was eager to explore something entirely different, for one should never be defined by a single dimension of personality or character.

It began one day at my home in an upstairs bedroom converted into an art studio. With brush in hand and a blank canvas on the easel, I tried something I'd never attempted before. I painted a picture, an abstract.

Splashes of color . . . swirling and sweeping across the empty whiteness . . . gaining momentum with each brush stroke. Until . . . a design emerges . . . imaginative, whimsical, delightful! I haven't had such fun in ages! The canvas explodes with life and joy! Beneath my fingertips, I have actually created something that was not there before, a part of myself I have never met.

In between conferences with new clients, appointments, and speaking engagements, I paint. I dip into a world peopled with the designs in my mind and spirit . . . free-flowing, luminous, translucent . . . or in brilliant hues of scarlet, indigo, gentian. Just naming those colors evokes the newborn artist in me.

Then one day, something different appears on the canvas beneath my brush. I blink. Shake my head. Blink again. There, before me, as if hovering in mid-flight, is an angel! Yes. Undeniably. An angel.

The words of a beloved Psalm flood my mind. The Lord seems to be saying, "I will hide you under My wings." These are the wings of the angel on my canvas. Thank You, God!

Since that day, I've begun to share my angel portraits with others. A young couple grieving the loss of their three-year-old daughter. The family of a woman with breast cancer, dying much too young at 42.

In sharing, my pleasure in the painting is multiplied.

Through the years, I have been aware of the Master Artist, sculpting and crafting my life, then sketching in the delicate details before applying the paint... the lights, the darks, the sunshine, the shadows. Sometimes I have felt the sting as some flaw in the work must be buffed away. You have them, too—the highlights, the lows, the moments of indescribable pain, the bursts of pure bliss. All the beauty in the world is contained in each of us. Splendid. Incomparably lovely. Unique.

We probably have more in common than you would imagine, you and I. Come sit with me, and let me tell you my story. And I want to hear yours, for this book is the journey of only *one* life.

As we walk together through the pages of my life, we will visit memories of my childhood and meet my parents—my father, who once saved me from death only to lose his own life prematurely. My mother, who struggled with health issues, yet provided a place of security and peace for her three children. A teacher who saw potential in me when others shut me out. Mentors who believed in me before I knew how to believe in myself. It was my mother, though, who was the first to instill in me the confidence that I could succeed.

But success does not come quickly, easily, or without a price tag. The biblical heroes I met as a child in a little country Sunday school often suffered for years before they ascended to greatness. For Abraham, there was a test of his faith—the willingness to sacrifice his beloved son Isaac— before he could become the "father of nations." For Joseph, there was a pit and a prison before there was a palace. For Mary, the mother of Jesus, there was the shame of an unplanned pregnancy before there was the glory of giving birth to the Son of God.

And for some, there were failures along the way. David, the sweet shepherd/songwriter of Israel, a man after God's own heart, succumbed to the temptation of lust. The prophet Jonah ran from God's call and was swallowed by a great fish, whose belly became the altar where Jonah repented. And Saul, who killed Christians, spent years away from the God he claimed to serve before encountering Jesus Christ on the road to Damascus. Only then did he fall on his face in a life-changing experience. Even these found their way back to God and His great plan for their lives.

Their stories help me tell *my* story. Their struggles help me understand *mine.* In each case, the Lord "spoke" to them—with an audible voice, through an angelic visitation, or in a dream. Most recently, He has spoken to me through my paintbrush.

Throughout this book, I will introduce you to the angels God has sent to guide me on my way. This great God who rescued our Bible friends also rescued me—and He can do the same for you. No matter what pit you've fallen into—or dug for yourself; no matter what evil forces have come against you, what temptation has overtaken you, or what disease has gripped your body, you can be an overcomer.

Even in pain, there is promise. In all the gray and golden moments of my life, I can attest that He has been faithful. He can take a broken heart, hold it close to His, and cause that heart to beat again. He can write a symphony with all the discordant notes of our failures. He can paint a Masterpiece on the dark canvas of our lives. He can use an unqualified CEO to lead a company to its knees and be successful beyond all dreams and expectations.

No doubt you think this book is going to be all about *me*. Not at all! This book is about God's work in and through a woman who realized she was nothing apart from Him. "As the Scriptures say, 'If you want to boast, boast only about the Lord'" (1 Corinthians 1:31).

My prayer is that, as my story unfolds, you may sense God at work in your own. If He speaks to you at some point, stop, listen, and savor the moment. Don't miss the blessing He has for you. For in all the tangled threads of our lives, the Master Weaver is creating a tapestry of exquisite beauty. And as our paths cross, who knows if He will weave us together in some intricate design that will change the course of both our lives.

He is with me on my journey; if you will ask Him, He will be with you on yours.

"ANGEL OF PRAISE"

Let everything that breathes sing praises to the Lord!
Praise the Lord!
PSALM 150:6

Chapter 1

The Secret Place

Those who live in the shelter of the Most High
will find rest in the shadow of the Almighty.
PSALM 91:1, NKJV

LOCATION. LOCATION. LOCATION. THE economy may be tanking, companies downsizing, and the job market shrinking, but our business is booming, and it's all about location. I was born for this industry: orchestrating the hopes of prospective homeowners in finding the home of their dreams in the right spot to meet their needs.

Having observed my mother's fledgling career in real estate, I tried my hand at sales early and found my niche. In later years, I moved into management and broke new ground, starting one company in 1988 and another in 2007. With no graduate degree or special training to my credit, however, I was forced to rely on my instincts—or so I thought.

In reality, the secret of my success is found in another location. Not in some lavish townhouse or country manor.

No sprawling estate or stately mansion. No, my secret is tucked away in my private refuge, the secret place.

I live in a lovely area of our fair city. A canopy of tall trees, their branches interlaced, shades the winding street. On prayer walks through my neighborhood, with the worship music of Michael W. Smith playing through my earphones, I am reminded of a green cathedral. Although our house is situated on a smaller lot, our backyard adjoins a polo field, which appears to stretch for miles. No one would imagine that this tranquil space could exist only twenty-six minutes from the bustling city of Atlanta. I love my home, but my true dwelling place is in the heart of God.

Each morning, in the sanctuary of my home, I feel God welcoming me into His throne room. With my Bible open and my heart tuned to hear His voice, I begin:

O Lord . . . Listen to my cry for help.
Pay attention to my prayer,
for it comes from honest lips.
PSALM 17:1

His Presence hovers near—perfect love, pure peace, amazing grace. All the heavy burdens of life in the corporate world fall away, and I rest.

I will wait quietly before [you],
for my victory comes from [you].
[You] alone [are] my rock and my salvation,
my fortress where I will never be shaken.
PSALM 62:1

People in this fast-paced society have forgotten how to be still. With cell phones glued to their ears and eyes on tablets and computer screens—all in the interest of faster and better communication—they pass by the very people who need their touch, eye contact, their *presence.*

Some years ago, I learned about giving God the first fruits of my time, money and energy—and resting in His presence. That's when I began an ongoing conversation with the Lover of my Soul, being careful to listen more and list my own issues or desires less. He never disappoints me.

Marie Chapian, in her wonderful devotional book, *God's Heart for You,* expresses beautifully in Scripture paraphrases, how our Father speaks to us. You'll read a quote from Marie at the end of each chapter of this book. For example, she draws from passages in the gospels of John and Mark to create a sentiment attributed to God in this poetic opening:

> I love to talk to you, I love to teach you, help you,
> guide you every minute you breathe.
> > Every hair on your head
> has a number. I know you. I know your going out
> and your coming in.
> > I am your Lord,
> and without Me you can do nothing.[1]

MOMENTS WITH THE MASTER

To keep my focus on Him, I have learned to use the ACTS method of prayer: Adoration, Confession, Thanksgiving, Supplication.[2]

Thinking of our mighty and merciful Father and all that He is, **praise and adoration** flow from my soul:

> *"Lord, who can compare with you?"* . . .
> *Give thanks to the Lord, for he is good!*
> *Who can list the glorious miracles of the Lord?*
> *Who can ever praise him enough?*
> PSALM 106:1–2

If all I do is focus on one aspect of His Personhood—His love, His faithfulness, His kindness—I could spend hours exalting Him. But considering His magnificent attributes, His purity and perfection brings me to my knees in recognition of my unworthiness:

> *Search me, O God, and know my heart;*
> *Test me and know my anxious thoughts.*
> *Point out anything in me that offends you*
> *And lead me along the path of everlasting life.*
> PSALM 139:23

Confession is the natural outcome of spending time with God. It helps me keep short accounts with Him. I try to be honest and vulnerable in acknowledging my sins. He already knows my faults; He simply asks me to agree with Him so He can forgive me quickly and restore our sweet relationship.

Thanksgiving comes next. That list continues to grow as I recount the myriad blessings that have been mine through the years. Not a day goes by that I don't thank God for the following:

My salvation—through Jesus Christ my Lord. Without it, I would never know the joy of eternal life with the Father in heaven . . . or His sweet, intimate presence here on earth.

My faith—without it, I would not be able to grasp the length and breadth and depth of His love for me . . . or face a future in bleak times.

My family—without them, I could not grow in giving and receiving love and forgiveness daily.

My health—He has healed me many times and brought me through the valley of cancer. I will praise Him as long as I live!

Protection—He has deployed warrior angels to guard and protect me and those I love. At the Name of Jesus, the Enemy has to flee.

Wisdom—He has given me insight for navigating troubled waters in these ever-darkening days and for meeting future challenges—at home and in the workplace.

Then I thank Him for answered prayer. I thank Him for healing two of my dear friends who were diagnosed with cancer but are now in remission. I thank Him for providing good jobs for some employees whom it was necessary to terminate. I thank Him for supernatural wisdom in all business and personal decisions. I sense that He has led with spot-on precision as the company has continued to evolve with the times.

> **Supplication** follows, presenting my petitions before the throne—the lost, the lonely, the left-outs, my great staff and the 350 agents representing us in the greater Atlanta area. And again, my precious family as I mention them by name. My husband, Bob, my chief encourager. Our two beautiful daughters— Stephanie and Susan. An amazing son-in-law, David, my business partner for the past eighteen years. And seven gorgeous grandchildren—Sarah, Ben, Abigail, Jack, Matthew, Emily, and Zach.

Pondering the problems of the young, I pause . . .

A close family member needs prayer, reminding me of myself many years ago. I, too, was off the path without a purpose. Arrogant. Impetuous. Strong-willed. Determined to do things *my* way. Having been there, I know so well the results of failing to heed godly wisdom.

Again, I wait . . .

In the stillness, I hear my Father's heartbeat. He knows us best and loves us with a love we can barely fathom. In that moment of desperation, I cry to Him: "Please help me! What can I do?"

The quiet impression comes quickly: *As My loving-kindness brings repentance, you also must be loving and non-*

judgmental. Say little, but go together into a courtroom and let the consequences of others' poor choices speak.

"Yes, Lord! I'll do it!"

Immediately, another voice intrudes, sly and insinuating. *Oh, you're much too busy for that. You have other commitments, remember? All of them are good works.*

Ha! I know *that* voice, too. "Oh, no you don't!" I reply. "This is someone dear to me, someone who needs me! I'll reschedule, delegate, whatever it takes to help!"

The answer to my passionate morning prayer comes only hours later when my cell phone signals an incoming text message. Miracle of miracles, it is the one who has been on my heart. Those few words to me are stunning: "Jenny, I need a job."

ROOM WITHOUT A VIEW

I'm a woman who likes to get things done in a timely manner. Having heard from the Lord specifically that morning, I wasted no time in arranging a meeting with this precious young person. In my office the next day, I felt a tiny surge of hope.

I explained that I was not hiring a "go-fer"—someone to run errands and do menial labor—but someone who wanted to learn the business.

"And just what will I be doing?"

"I want you to experience our marketing program firsthand. And you will be accompanying me to high-level meetings. But first, we have an appointment. There's someone I want you to meet."

Acting quickly on the Lord's instruction to introduce the harsh realities of life outside of His protection, I had called a friend who is a Superior Court judge and explained a bit about our situation. After asking him to impart some wisdom, he had invited us to visit his courtroom.

We arrived early, and to my surprise, we were ushered into the judge's private chambers. He gave us an hour and fifteen minutes of his time prior to convening the first session of the day.

"This is not a happy place," he began after we were comfortably seated. "You'll see people in shackles. They're here because they didn't make the right choices. Some of them will have a permanent address behind bars—a room without a view. But it doesn't have to end that way."

He paused and, over his spectacles, studied the pale face before him "You have a rich heritage. Any one of those prisoners you're going to see today would like to trade places with you. Jenny here has a sterling reputation as one of the most outstanding citizens of this city. She is revered in this community and beyond as a woman of great integrity and character. But it didn't come overnight. Her standing is the result of fifty years of making the right decisions at the right time, surrounding herself with good people, and seeking wisdom from above.

"A reputation takes many years to build. You have to earn respect and trust, but it only takes a fortnight or less to destroy that reputation. Reputation is what people think about you, but character is what the angels say about you before the throne of God."

Next to me, the blue eyes were as wide as saucers.

DIVINE DESIGN

Following our courtroom visit, I scheduled our new employee for the next few weeks as a part of our marketing department. My relative was a quick study in real estate. But, more importantly, I knew that, from the beginning, the Lord had a design for this life. "'I know the plans I have for You,' says the LORD, 'They are plans for good and not for disaster, to give you a future and a hope. . . . When you pray, I will listen. . . . [I will] bring you home again'" (Jeremiah 29:11-12, 14).

Learning to live in the secret place and listen to the Lord for ourselves is not easy. But He always promises to be there when we do. Meanwhile, it is my job to withhold judgment—freely embracing, loving unconditionally, and mentoring, not only in the details of the real estate business, but in providing direction to the dwelling place for that lonely heart. All that will remain is to unlock the door through prayer and walk in.

MANY MANSIONS

One of the items on our immediate agenda was the funeral of a friend who had been an agent with our company for several years. Ashley's premature death had come as a terrible shock to our corporate family and, of course, to her husband and son. It was my honor to deliver the eulogy.

What many of my friends and family may not know is that speaking before large crowds takes me outside my comfort zone. But when I share the Lord and the compassion and comfort His Holy Spirit brings, I could speak before multitudes. From the early hours I spend in His Presence, I draw from a deep well. And when I get up to speak, I know He will give me words of assurance and hope for those who are left behind.

On the morning of the funeral, my young protégée looked around the auditorium of the church, leaned over, and whispered, "Jenny, there are hundreds of people in this room. Aren't you scared?" (We later learned 700 people attended that day.)

I shrugged. "Numbers don't make any difference. The Spirit of God is with me."

At the appropriate time, I mounted the platform and stood at the podium to begin my tribute:

> When I spoke with Ashley for the last time, she reminded me to tell you she is at peace—no more pain and suffering—and that she loves the Lord. He is her Redeemer, her Refuge, her Rock, and her Shepherd.
>
> Earlier, when she realized that her time on earth was limited, she asked me to paint her an angel to stand by her bed. I was thrilled to do that small favor for her. The painting shows an angel holding a little lamb, much like the Good Shepherd was carrying Ashley.
>
> Life is fragile. We never know when God will draw a finish line across the path and call us into eternity. Ashley didn't know that, at 47, she would cross the finish line. Jesus tells us, "In my Father's house are many mansions. I go to prepare a place for you." I believe that our Lord has prepared a special place for our dear Ashley.
>
> We all need to think about our eternal destiny. It is our choice to accept God's provision or reject it. Just

as Jesus tells us in John 5:24: "I assure you, those who listen to my message and believe in God who sent me have eternal life." Ashley has passed from death into life. And we're here to celebrate the life she shared with each of us. But most of all, we celebrate her eternal life with God.

In closing, I read the lyrics from Don Wyrtzen's beautiful song about heaven;

Just think of stepping on shore and finding it heaven,
Of touching a hand and finding it God's.
Of breathing new air and finding it celestial.
Of waking up in glory and finding it Home.[3]

Throughout the tribute, I had noticed that my young relative's eyes had been riveted on me. I am praying that this dear one was listening—hearing with the heart.

ANGELS ALL AROUND US

I believe angels are listening, too, ready to do God's bidding—to guard and protect *us* and to glorify *Him.* Angels have always fascinated me. So much has been written about them in the Bible.

They appear in all the turning-point moments of Scripture: in the Old Testament--surrounding the throne of God in praise and guarding the Ark of the Covenant with their outspread wings; in the New Testament, heralding Jesus' birth, ministering to Him in the agony of Gethsemane, standing guard over His tomb, and making that glorious announcement on Resurrection morning: "He is not here! He is risen!"

THE PAINTINGS

Some time ago, a friend asked what I did in my spare time. What hobbies I enjoyed.

"Oh, I love to read," I replied, "and my husband and I do some traveling. . . . " But her question left me wondering if I had explored all my options.

Inspired by a North Carolina artist, Anne Neilson, and local artist, Melissa Payne Baker, I decided to try my hand at painting. That's when I visited an art store and bought a supply of canvases, acrylic paints, and brushes.

Even before the first lesson, I plunged in to express myself through art. At first, it was fun, dabbing on the paint in brilliant colors and smearing it on the canvas. But I found the exercise strangely unfulfilling until the Lord whispered in my spirit:

> *Paint the angels! Paint those angels I sent you when, as a child, you overheard your relatives planning to place you and your brother and sister in an orphanage— and I protected you. Paint those angels that carried you in their arms through the valley of cancer, and you thought you wouldn't make it—and I heard you. Paint those angels that were dispatched to guide you when you were sued by one of the richest men in the world, and you thought you would be destroyed—and I delivered you. Paint those angels!*

So I have. Angels of worship. Angels of praise. Angels of intercession. Guardian angels. Angels of mercy. Warrior angels. They've all become my dearest friends and companions.

Although we cannot always recognize them, angels intersect our lives as God directs and help us navigate all the ups and downs with greater ease.

* * *

I have been abundantly blessed. Financial stability in an uncertain economy. Success in the marketplace. Close family ties. Respect from my peers. Honors and accolades. A long and fruitful marriage. The favor of God. In this season of my life, I am enjoying an "embarrassment of blessings"!

But, as my judge friend reminded us in his chambers that day, "All this did not come overnight, but through hard work and the blessings and favor of God. It was built over many years."

ANGEL OF PRAISE

Praise Me in the silence of your night,
    praise Me in the crashing noon,
Praise Me in silence
    and in awe . . .
Your praise fills My heart.[4]

"ANGEL OF COURAGE"

Be strong and courageous!
Do not be afraid or discouraged.
For the LORD your God is with you wherever you go.
JOSHUA 1:9

Chapter 2

Touched by an Angel

I prayed to the Lord, and he answered me.
He freed me from all my fears. . . .
For the angel of the Lord is a guard; he surrounds and
defends all who fear him.
PSALM 34:4, 7

*I*N ATTEMPTING TO SORT out my story, the colors and textures of my life seem as tangled as the skeins of yarn in a knitting basket. I will do my best to be as transparent as possible, insofar as I can recall the past. Some memories are best left to gather dust.

My father was forty-nine and my mother twenty-nine when they met and married. Prior to their marriage, my dad lived in an exclusive private club in downtown Atlanta—Capital City Club—with other bachelors. With no wife or family, he immersed himself in his commercial roofing business, an enterprise that landed him two of the largest bids ever won in the Southeast—Bell Bomber Plant (now Lockheed, a plant that manufactured airplanes during World War II) in Marietta, and Rich's Department

Store downtown—widely known for its Pink Pig train at Christmas; its "Fashionata," the Southeast's most famous fashion show, produced and directed by Sol Kent, and its wonderful Magnolia Tea Room.

When he was not working, Daddy spent time at his country home—forty-two acres of lush Georgia pastureland, where white-faced Herefords grazed contentedly and several orchards produced fruit in abundance. Here he brought his bride in the summers to begin their life together. For the remainder of the year, their address was 3449 Peachtree Road in the city.

My parents proceeded to produce three children in the first ten years. We were born "with a silver spoon in our mouth," but the silver would tarnish as time rolled by.

ANGELS ON OVERTIME

For a few years in the sun-kissed Georgia summers, we were a happy family—my mother and father, my little sister Jackie, my baby brother Sandy, and me. We breathed the sweet country air, gathered eggs from the henhouse, and romped about like the white-faced calves in the meadow. We enjoyed shuffleboard, games of tag and hide 'n' seek, and fabulous barbecues, where Daddy presided over the grill. As I am writing, I can almost smell the steak sizzling on the fire pit.

In the orchard, we picked ripe peaches, biting into the luscious fruit and letting the juice dribble down our chins and onto our dresses and Sandy's little suits. In those carefree days, Mother didn't seem to mind. Annabelle, our household manager and nanny, could take out the stains with a little Clorox.

About half a mile from the main house, Daddy had dammed a small lake, fed by a babbling brook, to form a swimming pool. The three of us, along with the dozens of aunts, uncles, and cousins who often gathered there, splashed in the icy water, oblivious to the declining economy, the World War that was coming to a close, and my father's encroaching illness. Young and unaware, my siblings and I reveled in those days of innocence, shielded from harm by a Heavenly Father we had not yet come to know, but who must have daily dispatched His angels to rescue us.

My darling baby brother was a delight, but he required a constant watchful eye. At two and a half, he was fearless. So fearless, in fact, that once he dared to climb under a fence enclosing the pasture where our Hereford cows and a bull were grazing.

Advancing happily toward the animals, waving his little fists and holding a red cloth like a miniature matador, Sandy caught the bull's attention. Had it not been for Prince, our protective German Shepherd, my brother might not be here to tell his story. Sensing the imminent danger, Prince leaped into action and cleared the fence just in time to pull Sandy to safety—by the seat of his pants!

As he grew, so did his curiosity, which often resulted in trouble, None of us will ever forget the time Sandy almost bled to death. Out in the well house, Annabelle's husband, West, who took care of things on the farm, had left a long pipe he used for cleaning the well. Intrigued by the shiny pole, Sandy grabbed the pipe. Nearby was an empty broken five-gallon glass water jug. Somehow, he lost his balance and tumbled, falling on the jug and gashing his upper arm on a jagged shard. Blood spurted everywhere! Sandy cried. Jackie screamed. I took charge. My critical thinking skills were developed early—out of necessity.

Mother was away, so I sent Jackie to get Annabelle, who wrapped a towel around the injured arm and applied pressure. We then called the Gantts, who drove us to the nearest doctor's office to stitch up the wound. To this day, Sandy has the scar to prove it. And I have his sweet commendation tucked away in my memory: "Jenny is a leader," he told a friend of mine recently. "She always puts the well-being of others first. She took over that day, and her quick thinking probably saved my life."

ANOTHER CLOSE CALL

And then there was an incident at our improvised swimming pool when I was seven. While our parents were entertaining friends and relatives on a balmy summer evening, Sandy jumped into the deep end. Of course, he couldn't swim and soon he was thrashing about in distress. One of our female cousins, Roberta, fished him out before any real damage was done.

Not long afterward, this scene was replayed. That time, it was *I* who was fighting for my life.

While the days were long and delicious, friends and family had gathered for yet another festive occasion. Daddy was grilling sirloin strip steaks, and plumes of hickory smoke rose in the air, tempting the appetite with the promise of the good food to come. Our guests were chatting while Mother completed dinner preparations and the children splashed in the pool.

In the merriment, no one noticed when three young

neighbor boys ducked me under the water. They didn't see my blond head bobbing or hear my muffled cries for help.

Apparently, the mischievous boys, only two or three years older than I, decided to "see how long she can hold her breath!" They didn't bother to ask if I could swim, and since I couldn't, how was I supposed to know to hold my breath when submerged!

If my father had not looked up from his grill at that moment, the CPR he performed might not have revived me. I never knew what happened to the boys. Sobered by the frightening scene as all of the grown-ups hovered over me, watching Daddy attempt to clear my lungs of water, they must have made a hasty departure and were not seen around our place again.

I have often thought how my Heavenly Father spared my life that day. He knew the plans He had for me—"plans to give me a future and a hope." Still, no doubt our guardian angels had to work overtime, or we would not have survived childhood.

PRECIOUS MEMORIES

While summers in those days were long and lazy, other seasons were absolutely magical. Christmas, especially. Winters in the South did not resemble a Currier and Ives Christmas card, of course. Rarely did we have snow in December, but that didn't deter us from celebrating in fine style.

When it was time to select the perfect tree to decorate for the holidays, we went out to the farm. Somewhere in the wooded area behind the house, we would be sure to find the most beautiful evergreen, most often a lush cedar.

Daddy would cut down the tree, and West, or one of the other caretakers on the property, would throw it over his shoulder and load it into our station wagon. Or, if our parents had decided to spend the holidays at the farm, he would set up the tree on a stand in the farmhouse.

Once the tree was situated in the living room, we would gather around the kitchen table to craft the items that would adorn its fragrant branches. There were popcorn and cranberries for stringing, paper chains of red and green, and hundreds of colored lights. Then, when the tree was heavy with our handmade ornaments, Daddy would turn on the lights, and we would gasp in delight.

Each Christmas Eve, there was the reading of the beloved poem, "The Night Before Christmas." As Mother read, Jackie, Sandy, and I were convinced we could hear Rudolph and his companions prancing and pawing on the roof, bringing Santa's sleigh to our house for a Christmas delivery. We were careful to leave cookies and milk for his midnight snack before we went to bed, much too excited to sleep!

One Christmas when we were young, Jackie and I spied something in Macy's Department Store that we both wanted desperately. It was an aqua, velvet-lined musical jewelry box, complete with a tiny lock and key for keeping our treasures safe. We had hinted to our mother that this was at the top of our lists, hardly daring to dream that they might really be ours. But on Christmas morning that year, we found two of those beautifully wrapped boxes under our tree!

Another highlight of the season was Annabelle's

Christmas brunch, when she served fried chicken with all the fixin's. Nobody fried chicken like Annabelle.

Close behind Christmas in my gallery of memories was Easter. One Easter Eve, Mother stayed up all night at her Singer sewing machine, finishing some darling white organza pinafores for Jackie and me. She must have been exhausted when Easter morning dawned, but we were thrilled with our pretty new dresses.

* * *

Daddy was usually a part of our family activities. More and more often, though, he was absent, either working in town at his place of business—the Sanford Roofing Company—or lying in bed after arriving home, pale and tired. We would not know until later the true nature of his condition.

When winter melted into spring and spring blossomed into summer again, to while away the long afternoons on the farm, Jackie, Sandy, and I played in an old Army trailer-turned-schoolhouse. Being the oldest and bossiest, I, of course, was the teacher, and they, my students. Little did I know how prophetic those early classroom sessions would be.

I taught my younger brother and sister whatever subjects struck my fancy, issuing commands with all the authority and brass of a drill sergeant. I also instructed them in matters of the heart. Two of the Bible verses never left our collective memories:

You are the light of the world—like a city on a hilltop that cannot be hidden. . . .

In the same way, let your good deeds shine out for all to see,
so that everyone will praise your heavenly Father.
MATTHEW 5:14, 16

Those words, too, would prove prophetic for me.

CLIMBING THE LADDER

Many years later, a counselor told me, "Your childhood ended when you were eight years old." That was the year my father died, leaving his widow with a pile of debt and three children. I was the oldest; Jackie was five and Sandy, three. Despite his earlier success, by now the financial picture was quite grim.

Torn between taking care of us at home or providing the necessities of life, Mother had no choice but to take over the roofing business. In a day when few women ventured outside the home to work and even fewer owned a business, this was indeed a strange new world.

In the last three months of his illness, Daddy had done his best to instruct our mother in the day-to-day management of the company. But there was still so much to learn—how to bid for a job, hire employees, cut payroll, maintain general accounting, etc. A major requirement of the job was the inspection of roofs, both before and after the work was completed. Daddy had failed to mention that this involved climbing ladders. My mother had never climbed a ladder in her life, let alone a ladder tall enough to reach the roof of a two-story building!

One of her first contracts after assuming control of the company was a large warehouse on the outskirts of town. A severe thunderstorm had swept through the area, leaving roof damage from golf-ball-sized hail. It was her job to assess the damage and estimate the cost before calling in a repair crew.

She arrived at the site about mid-morning on a hot July day, wearing what any well-dressed woman of her day would wear for warm-weather activities–a casual dress and "sensible" shoes. Unfortunately, it was hardly the appropriate attire for climbing ladders.

But she gathered her courage and made the climb, her skirts billowing about her legs. There was absolutely no way she could smooth them down since she had to hold onto the ladder with both hands. Looking on from below were the warehouse owner and several workmen. I can only imagine how Mother, a modest Southern lady, must have felt.

Determined to get the job done, she bravely mounted the last few rungs of the ladder and stepped out onto the flat tar roof. Heat waves shimmered off the hot roofing in the blazing sun, almost scorching her feet in her thin-soled shoes.

Making a quick assessment of the damage, she descended the ladder as gracefully as possible. By the time she was safely back on the ground, she had made her first executive decision. From this day forward, she would delegate this phase of the operation to one of her managers.

The paperwork was not much easier. With only a few years of formal education, Mother was ill prepared to handle all the details of running a company. It was a good thing she could rely on Annabelle to manage the household, with West keeping up with the farm chores.

* * *

Our little world rocked on in this way for a while. Leaving the three of us in the capable hands of Annabelle and West, Mother braved the unfamiliar world of business, but often came home drained and exhausted. Noticing her sad face, we three children put our heads together to concoct creative ways to lift her spirits. We put on little plays and skits, rehearsing for hours to ensure a stellar performance. Her occasional smile was reward enough.

With the approach of Mother's Day one year, I had a bright idea! I would convince my brother and sister to "contribute" their school lunch money, and we would pool our resources to buy her a special gift. What I didn't count on was Jackie and Sandy telling Annabelle on me.

"Jenny takes all our lunch money every day, and we're hungry!" they wailed.

Annabelle tattled to Mother, and I got a whipping with a peach tree switch that she made me cut from the tree myself. I never told her why I had taken the children's money, and my little heart was broken.

Eventually, the roofing business, left so heavily in debt by my ailing father, began to fail. Unbeknownst to my mother, he had signed the farm and our 42 acres over to the company, and back taxes had accrued.

In the throes of this crisis, the final straw occurred when an experienced, capable man, who had been with Daddy from the beginning—Mother's brother-in-law—left suddenly, after receiving a large bonus from her. Ironically, he used the bonus to start his own company. His departure precipitated an estrangement with certain members of our family that lasted for several years. Apparently, he didn't enjoy taking orders from a woman, and my poor mother had to endure yet another nail in the coffin.

When both the house and the farm were sold at auction on the courthouse steps, we were devastated. It was the beginning of a long, dark winter.

"DEAR GOD, I'M SO AFRAID!"

Putting the furniture in storage and gathering our belongings, we moved in temporarily with one of Mother's five sisters who lived in Decatur. My aunt took care of Mother, who was fragile and whose "nervous" condition had worsened, and I supervised the care of my little brother and sister. While I was truly concerned about my mother's continuing downward spiral, I relished my new role as caregiver and boss of our dwindling family. That is, until the night I overheard a conversation in the hallway outside the room I shared with my mother.

She had been unresponsive for weeks, just sitting in a chair and staring straight ahead without uttering a word. My aunt was horrified that her sister might die before her eyes. Apparently, one night, the situation got the best of my aunt, and she collapsed in tears.

"We can't go on like this," I heard my aunt tell my uncle. "She's no better, in spite of all that medicine the doctor is giving for depression. And you know this house wasn't built to hold seven children—our four and her three."

My uncle didn't say anything, and I held my breath, waiting to hear how he would answer. He sighed. "You're right. I can't have you all torn up this way, and we can't afford to take care of them much longer. . . . I'm thinking she would be better off in a mental institution anyway . . . where they could try some of those shock treatments on her."

I had heard about those treatments. They seemed bizarre and barbaric. I shuddered, thinking how my helpless mother might be hooked up to some kind of horrible machine with wires attached to her head—a scene straight out of *Frankenstein*.

"And maybe we ought to call the Methodist Children's Home, too. . . . " he continued, his voice trailing off at the thought.

"I've already called them," I heard my aunt reply in a quavering voice, "but they can't take but two of the children. We'd have to find a place for the third. It's a shame they'd have to be separated, but I don't know what else to do."

I didn't wait to hear more. I slid out of bed, careful not to wake Mother. It was the very first time that I had ever prayed anything more than a "Now-I-lay-me-down-to-sleep" or a "God-is-great, God-is-good" kind of prayer. It was time to pound on the gates of heaven and plead. I couldn't bear the thought of losing the rest of my family. My mother just *had* to get well!

Sobbing, I poured out my heart: "Dear God, please heal my mother! I'm so afraid we'll be separated—my brother and sister and me! You've got to do something. Please?" When I finally dried my tears and climbed back into bed, it must have been around ten o'clock. Mother hadn't moved, and I fell into a restless sleep.

Sometime in the middle of the night, I was startled awake by a strange sound. Someone was shuffling around in the room. Then I heard a voice. For the first time in six months, my mother was talking! I had never seen her pick up a Bible, but I recognized some of the words from Psalm 23 in the old King James English:

The LORD is my shepherd; I shall not want.
He maketh me to lie down in green pastures:
He leadeth me beside the still waters.
He restoreth my soul . . .
Yea, though I walk through the valley of the shadow
of death, I will fear no evil:
For thou art with me . . .
Surely goodness and mercy shall follow me
all the days of my life:
And I will dwell in the house of the LORD forever.

Getting out of bed, I followed close behind as Mother paced the floor. While she was reciting those timeless words, I was praising God for answering my prayer! And thus began her slow recovery from deep darkness.

IN THE HOUSE OF THE LORD

Many years later, after we had all left home to pursue marriage and careers and Mother was battling diabetes, we became increasingly concerned about her welfare. One incident of diabetic coma that sent her to the emergency room convinced us that she could no longer live alone. My husband and I gladly brought her home to live with us. That decision proved a wise one as it would mark the last year of her life.

One evening, I felt compelled to go to her bedroom and ask a most significant question. "Mother," I began, "if you died today, would you know for sure that you would be in heaven with God?"

"Why, I certainly hope so." She seemed puzzled that I would ask. "I've tried to be a good person."

"Yes, Mother, you've certainly survived unbelievable circumstances in your life. So many admire you, and we all love you. But there's only one way to know that you will be in heaven for all eternity." In the next few minutes, I presented the plan of salvation.

* * *

In years to come, others would ask me how they could know for certain that they would be in heaven when they die. It's so simple that children can come to the Lord—once they understand that we have all sinned and need a Savior.

For if you confess with your mouth that Jesus is Lord
and believe in your heart that God raised him from the dead,
you will be saved.
For it is by believing in your heart that you
are made right with God,
and it is by confessing with your mouth that you are saved.
ROMANS 10:9–10

So simple. So profound. So utterly life-changing!

One woman explains it this way: "I once accidentally left a purple crayon in the pocket of my four-year-old son's jeans. When I ran the jeans through the washer and dryer, you can imagine what happened! I couldn't remove the purple crayon stain. All the clothes were ruined. I cried in frustration.

"It was at this particular moment that the Holy Spirit decided to speak to me about the love of God. He gave me a hint of the great despair my Heavenly Father felt over my soul—and yours—being forever ruined by the indelible stain of sin. . . . My cleanliness before our Holy God is a gift from Him paid for by the blood of His only Son. A gift I did not earn. Nor do I deserve it. My stains are gone."[1]

★ ★ ★

It was words like these I shared with my mother that day. I waited for her response. When she was silent, I pressed her a little, "Would you like to pray a prayer accepting Jesus as your Savior?"

"Yes, Jenny, I would."

I knelt beside her bed. Mother was too frail to get on her knees, so I took both her hands in mine and led her in a prayer of salvation. She repeated the words after me in her whispery voice:

"O God, I come to You just as I am. I am willing to turn from my sins and receive Your Son Jesus as my Lord and Savior. From this moment on, I want to follow Him, and I surrender my life to Him. Have Your own way, Lord. In Christ's Name, amen."

It's just as simple as John 3:16: "For God loved the world so much that he gave his one and only Son, so that everyone who believes in him will not perish but have eternal life."

When Mother left us to "dwell in the house of the Lord forever" three months later, I was so thankful we'd had this all-important conversation.

THE TOUCH

While our mother loved us dearly—teaching us to mind our manners, to speak when we were spoken to, and to do our best in whatever we undertook—she neglected to instruct us in spiritual matters. On the other hand, our nearest neighbors, the Gantts, who lived over a mile from our old home place in the country, never missed a Sunday attending the Sardis Baptist Church and often invited our family to go with them. Mother always declined, saying she was too exhausted from her long work week. But Sunday mornings with the Gantts soon became the highlight of my life.

Every week they stopped by in their Model T to pick us up—at least, those of us who were willing to go. I tried all my tricks with my brother and sister to rouse them early on those mornings and get them ready for church. I prepared their breakfast, pleaded, cajoled, and even threatened them with demerits, but it was usually only my sister Jackie who reluctantly came along. Sandy generally stayed behind with our mother. I, on the other hand, could not wait to get to that little country church.

Like a honeybee to a morning glory, I was drawn to the sweet aroma of my Savior. He was tugging at my heartstrings, wooing me, even as a child of ten. All I knew at the time was that I wanted to go to church with the Gantts more than I wanted anything else on earth.

There I heard joyful songs, heartfelt prayer, and "Bible words" from the preacher—words that seemed to penetrate the deepest parts of my tender heart, a place that had never been touched in just that way before. Everything in me hungered for the One who said He loved me more than anyone had ever loved me, and when the preacher gave the altar call the very first Sunday, I hurried down the aisle to "give my heart to Jesus."

The next Sunday and the next, feeling that the Lord Himself—or maybe an angel—had tapped me on the shoulder, I went forward again.

By the third Sunday, the pastor seemed puzzled. When I reached the front of the church where he was standing to receive those who were making a commitment, he leaned over and whispered in my ear, "My dear, you've already given your heart to Jesus. You don't have to come to the altar *every* Sunday."

Cupping my mouth with my hand, I whispered back, "I just wanted to make sure!"

What followed are memories that remain as fresh as yesterday. Among them are the fabulous dinners-on-the-ground for which that particular denomination was famous. All the ladies of the church—fine country cooks, every one—would bring their most mouth-watering casseroles, platters mounded high with fried chicken, barbecued ribs still simmering in sauce, vegetables fresh from the farm, cornbread, biscuits, homemade rolls, and an endless array of delectable desserts—enough scrumptious pies and cakes and cookies to satisfy every sweet tooth in the congregation. I had no trouble persuading my brother and sister to attend church with me on those special Sundays!

It was my newfound joy in Jesus and regularly spending time with others who felt the same way that anchored me during that difficult time.

"SWEET GEORGIA BROWN"

Later, as I became a teenager and entered a frightening and unexplored phase of life—my high school years—I drifted from my moorings and began to feel insecure. Maybe it was because, without a home of our own for a while, we moved from relative to relative, never able to put down roots. In fact, we children graced the halls of three schools in three years.

As a newcomer many times over, it was difficult enough to break in to the school cliques. But observing that most of the girls were wearing the latest fashion fads was devastating! It wasn't that I didn't have nice clothes. It was the *sweaters* the other girls wore. Honestly, in my adolescent fantasy, I thought every one of those girls must have at least twenty cashmere sweaters in her closet.

Now that Mother was well again, she was doing her best to keep our family afloat by taking any job she could find—selling children's encyclopedias door to door and, more recently, working as a secretary at a realty company. I didn't want to burden her, but she knew I was dying to have one of those sweaters.

I don't know how she did it, but she managed to scrape together enough money to surprise me one day with my heart's desire. The sweater was baby blue cashmere, with a white collar. I was in heaven. I'll never forget what she told me that day as she took me in her arms and held me close. "Honey, you're so smart. I know that someday you'll be able to have all the cashmere sweaters you want."

Well, I never felt very smart. But her unshakable

confidence in me did as much to boost my morale as the unexpected gift. We might have been struggling, but none of us ever doubted our mother's love.

Another who believed in me was my Social Studies teacher. She must have noticed that I was never nominated for any class honors or offices, so she took it upon herself to appoint me as a member of the chorus line in our high school musical, "Sweet Georgia Brown." All those popular girls . . . and me. Her encouragement was vital to my survival during those bleak days.

Feeling lost and left out and yearning for more, I graduated with the rest of my class. Many of them were making their plans to enter college in the fall. With limited funds, there were no such long-term plans for me, although Mother had saved enough to send me to a quarter or two of college before switching over to business school. Beyond that, I had not the slightest idea what I would do with the rest of my life. But I could dream . . .

ANGEL OF COURAGE

Be strong and of good courage!
Trials are also gifts from Me,
changing you from one glory
to another. Never shrink back from your
high calling as an overcomer.[2]

"Angel of Love"

The Lord is . . . filled with unfailing love.
Psalm 103:8

Chapter 3

Looking for Love

I have loved you . . . with an everlasting love;
With unfailing love I have drawn you to myself.
JEREMIAH 31:3

*I*N THE 1950s, THAT era of innocence, every young
girl dreamed of getting married someday. I was
no exception. My husband-to-be would be tall and
handsome, we would fall madly in love, and I would
walk down the aisle, wearing a gorgeous wedding gown
like Elizabeth Taylor in "Father of the Bride." There
would be no more loneliness, no rejection, no financial
worries, no feeling less than acceptable. My new
husband would *adore* me, and we would live happily
ever after.

I don't know where I ever got such notions. Maybe
these ideas came from reading movie-star magazines
and romantic novels, or from the movies I saw at the
Buckhead Theater, or the television programs that were
all the rage—"The Donna Reed Show," "Leave it to
Beaver," and the Christmas special "It's a Wonderful

Life" that we watched on our black-and-white TV. Wasn't life *supposed* to be wonderful when you were married and had a home of your own?

COLLEGE OR CAMELOT?

In those lean times, Mother was a *single parent* before that term was coined. Holding down a job at the real estate company while monitoring the activities of three teenagers was challenging. While I was home, I tried to help her by corralling my siblings, feeling that old maternal instinct where their well-being was concerned. But I was getting tired of that role. It was time to move on and live my own life.

With a little business college behind me, at least I would be prepared to become a secretary to some businessman somewhere, as was the custom of so many girls in that day. That is, unless I got a better offer.

Marriage seemed remote, though. The boys I dated in high school were hopelessly young and immature. However, when a friend introduced me to a debonair older man—he was 31, older than I by ten years—I was immediately interested. Perhaps he held the key to what my heart longed for—security.

He called. I answered. Dinner at Camelia Gardens in Buckhead sounded divine, and I took extra pains getting ready for our first date. I styled my blond shoulder-length hair in a glamorous pageboy and put on a dress that swished around my ankles in case he took me dancing afterward.

At dinner, his charm and easy-going personality masked any potential threat to our budding relationship.

More dates followed. Our friendship blossomed into what I just knew had to be true love, and we were married within the year. Innocent and vulnerable, I did not suspect that he would crush those tender petals, one by one.

The character flaws that had only surfaced occasionally during our year of courtship—control, self-centeredness, anger—were exacerbated after marriage. The result was emotional and physical abuse. One counselor warned me that, because of my husband's tendency to dominate through intimidation, he could harm me . . . and by now, I had someone else to consider—I was pregnant.

As my rose-colored dream faded into nightmarish reality, my first child, Stephanie, was born. She was the only joy I experienced during that ill-fated marriage.

After our daughter's birth, my husband's dark side grew darker. He had always been opinionated and self-centered, but now he became even more so. He was demanding and expected my attention constantly, even though I was caring for a newborn, was sleep-deprived and was recovering from childbirth.

I was miserable. I felt a little like the biblical hero Joseph must have felt in the early days of his imprisonment as a captive in the land of Egypt. He had been sold into slavery by his own brothers—the very people who should have loved and protected him. I wasn't locked in a physical prison during my marriage, and certainly not for nearly as long as Joseph, but I felt emotionally trapped, constantly degraded and humiliated by my husband, the one who should have loved me most.

I didn't consult the Lord at this point. My husband

and I had not been in a Bible-believing church, nor had I sought any Christian friends or wisdom from church leaders. But things couldn't go on like this. It was almost as if my husband were thinking, *If I can't have her, nobody can have her.* Mind-numbing.

With my husband's fiery temper, combined with his drinking problem, I was legitimately concerned about our safety; so I consulted a counselor. The counselor had warned me that, in a drunken rage, my husband might be dangerous, and strongly advised me to file for divorce and move far away. I took his advice and filed, but I was reluctant to leave my family, all of whom still lived in Atlanta.

Since I knew the counselor was probably right, I did make up my mind to move out of our home. While my husband was out of town and with the help of my sister-in-law, I packed up exactly half of the furnishings—one chair for me, one chair for him; a table lamp for me, a floor lamp for him—and moved into an apartment. It was a fair exchange, I reasoned. He would get the house and half of the furniture in return for my freedom.

After my divorce was final, I was sad, but relieved. I also felt the old demon of fear rising to haunt me. The honeymoon was long over. Now I would have to try to make a new life for myself and my child. The thing I had always dreaded most was upon me. I was alone again.

Except for my job as an administrative assistant to an executive in an oil company, my eighteen-month-old daughter Stephanie and I would be starting over with practically nothing. The judge had awarded minimal child support, and reality quickly set in. What were we to do? How was I going to make it? Only the Lord knew, and He and I weren't on speaking terms these days.

A NEW BEGINNING

Working in the financial department at Tennessee Corporation, a division of Cities Service Oil Company, was a brilliant young financial analyst, Bob Pruitt. I had noticed him when passing by his door on my way to run an errand for my boss. Bob would always look up when he saw me coming, and I couldn't help noticing that he seemed interested.

Later, a co-worker reported that Bob had "checked me out" and had learned that I was newly divorced and was not dating anyone—yet. Hmm. Maybe I should do some checking of my own.

After a few well-placed inquiries, I learned that Bob hailed from Savannah, was a graduate of Georgia Tech, had lots of fun friends from his Chi Phi fraternity, and had never been married. Nice résumé, so far. But I wanted to know more.

My opportunity came when I was invited to a get-together after work one Friday night. To unwind from the intense pace of the workweek, some of the single employees would gather to socialize on weekends at someone's apartment. A friend of Bob's was throwing the party on this particular evening, and this time, Bob and I ran into each other under more relaxed circumstances.

With soft background music on the record player, he asked me to dance. In his arms, the sparks flew instantly. To my surprise, Bob told me that he had met me before—two years earlier. I was married at the time and working at Lenox Towers. He was employed by a local bank and had dropped by to call on someone in my building. He had not forgotten that first meeting.

Conversation flowed freely, and I learned how much we had in common. Bob might have had a genteel Southern upbringing, but the circumstances of his childhood were similar to mine. As the hours ticked by, he shared with me that his mother, too, had been widowed, with three children to raise. I felt an immediate bond.

After that night, we saw each other often. Formal dating soon evolved into a deep friendship. He would drop by the apartment after work and ask what I wanted to do. With Stephanie now a toddler, we usually settled for a home-cooked meal that we would prepare together. After I put Stephanie to bed, Bob and I would sit down to watch a movie on TV.

Six months into the relationship, I knew he was the one for me. He was kind, gentle, thoughtful, a man of integrity and loyalty—all the qualities my first husband had lacked. My mind was made up. But being a careful analyst, Bob was not quick to make decisions. He had to think things through.

"I THOUGHT YOU'D NEVER ASK!"

Time was moving on, but not Bob. After a year and a half of dating, I was beginning to think he was a confirmed bachelor and had no intention of asking me to marry him.

Once I sent myself some flowers and signed the card: "From Your Secret Admirer." That elicited a little curiosity from Bob, but no proposal.

Finally, just before Memorial Day, I made a serious

move. When Bob asked what "we" were planning for the holiday weekend, I replied, "I don't know about *you,* but *I'm* planning a trip to the beach with some girlfriends."

He looked stunned.

When I returned to work the next Monday, tanned and glowing, my blond hair highlighted by the sun, I asked Bob, "How was your weekend?"

"Not very good." He was clearly miserable.

It wasn't long before he was inundating me with phone calls, asking me for dates—breakfast, lunch, and dinner . . . out. So I wasn't too surprised when he asked me to have dinner with him at Camelia Gardens, the location of my first date with my ex.

But that memory quickly faded when Bob reached across the table for my hand. "I have something to ask you." I held my breath. "I can't take a chance on losing you. Will you marry me?"

With that, he produced a card and a jeweler's ring box. The card read: "This diamond is not huge, but it matches the sparkle in your blue eyes."

It was my turn to be stunned.

We were married on October 29, 1966. When I walked down the aisle on that crisp, fall day to wed the love of my life, I thought my heart would explode with happiness. And now, forty-nine years later, when he walks into a room, my heart still skips a beat. *Most* days.

SETTLING DOWN/MOVING UP

For a year after we were married, Bob and I continued to work at Cities Service. Then I landed a better position with a group of commercial real estate brokers affiliated with a residential construction company. Surrounded by professionals in the housing industry and the excitement of pairing people with the places where they would likely spend some of the most significant years of their lives, my interest was at an all-time high.

My mother had encouraged me to get into real estate sales, and now Bob was echoing her advice. But I knew I didn't test well, and I wasn't sure I had what it took to pass the real estate boards. Bob promised to help me.

I had known that my husband was smart before I married him. That was one of the reasons I was attracted to him in the first place. I didn't realize just *how* smart until I had a chance to take the real estate course. He coached me all the way through, drilling me on mortgages and liens, escrow and closing costs. I could never have made it without him. In due time, thanks to Bob, I passed the boards.

ROCK STAR OF REAL ESTATE

Quite by accident, I discovered that sales was my sweet spot. While I was working for the commercial brokers, my boss Bobby Wright called me to staff a house one weekend, filling in for an agent who was unable to make it. I wasn't expecting to do more than show up, answer a few questions, and resume my weekend activities. But the first couple loved the house and didn't need to look any further. They were ready to purchase that day. Monday morning, the paperwork was on my boss's desk. He was astonished, but no one was more surprised than I.

The next weekend was a repeat of the first. Again, I showed a house and the prospective buyers . . . bought!

By this time, Bobby Wright was bewildered. He had sent an inexperienced young woman to the properties simply to direct all but the most basic inquiries to the home office on Monday morning, when a *real* agent would be available. In fact, he had instructed me *not* to ask for the order.

I had started with no intention of closing any deals, but the art of making sales is a delicate dance. When I observed those prospective homebuyers taking the first step—watched them measure the rooms to see if their furniture would fit, heard them discuss wallpaper and paint—I just couldn't resist following their lead, and asked: "Would you like to write a contract?" You already know the answer.

An agent listens with the heart, and as the magical moment presents itself, he or she moves with the music. Honestly, that's all I did on those weekends. I later learned that I had recognized what is called "buying signals."

The new homeowners remarked, "It was a most pleasant experience."

Bobby Wright told me, "You have a servant spirit."

I put it down to doing what came naturally—following a calling God had placed on my heart from the beginning.

Suddenly, another rare memory of earlier days surfaced—the time when, as a child living in Buckhead, I had sold more Girl Scout cookies than any other girl in the state of Georgia. Maybe I was destined for sales. The product might be different—houses and condos were not quite the same as cookies—but the motivation was the same: to be the best I could be.

With my license, my newly honed skills, and plenty of

confidence, I decided to approach the most prestigious real estate company in Atlanta, Northside Realty and Associates, to inquire about becoming an agent. I knew they only kept an active list of about thirty agents in that office and quickly learned that they had reached their quota.

Not one to give up easily and with Bob cheering me on, I drafted a letter to Northside. "I hear that there's no room in the inn," I began with a hint of humor. "But if I came on board with business in tow, would you hire me?"

It seemed that no sooner had my letter reached Northside's corporate headquarters than I received a call from one of their brokers. "I think we should talk."

I wasted no time in making an appointment and arrived promptly at the scheduled hour, dressed for success. True to my word, I provided half a million dollars' worth of listings. *Very* impressed, the broker hired me on the spot, and I was on my way!

Mentored by one of the top agents in Atlanta, Skipper Morrison, I learned more about the servant's heart toward my clients that Bobby Wright had recognized. (Much more about that later.) Nothing was too much to ask of her. Since I loved people, Skipper's strategy seemed a perfect fit.

Life was sweet. My career was off the charts, and when we learned I was expecting again, we were ecstatic. In 1969, the second year of my real estate career, all my dreams were fulfilled as we welcomed a second precious daughter, Susan.

By the third year, I made the Million Dollar Club. As one of their up-and-coming young agents, in 1970 I sold the highest-priced property in Atlanta—a Howard Chatham home in River Shore Estates—that closed at $99,500. That would be something like a million dollars today.

With this taste of real success and the applause and accolades that accompanied it, I was unstoppable. I became the rock star of residential real estate, and I spent the next few years building my career. Away from the company of other Christians and out of touch with the Lord, I didn't realize I was building my house on *sand*.

Maybe you know the story. Jesus told this parable in Matthew 7:24-27:

> *Anyone who listens to my teaching and follows it is wise,*
> *like a person who builds a house on solid rock.*
> *Though the rain comes in torrents and the floodwaters rise*
> *and the winds beat against that house,*
> *it won't collapse because it is built on bedrock.*
> *But anyone who hears my teaching and ignores it is foolish,*
> *like a person who builds a house on sand.*
> *When the rains and floods come and the winds beat*
> *against that house,*
> *it will collapse with a mighty crash.*

Living my fairytale existence, I was blissfully unaware that I was setting myself up for a "mighty crash."

HEART SURGERY

Recently, my cardiologist recommended a procedure that would restore proper rhythm to my heart. Having been diagnosed with a rather common condition known as A-Fib (atrial fibrillation), I had experienced episodes of heart palpitations and irregular heartbeats—some so severe that

I had to lie down frequently. Not pleasant nor conducive to productivity—at work or at home.

Before going to the hospital, I happened to read a great devotional by Max Lucado, who described his own A-Fib as "a heartbeat with the regularity of a telegraph operator sending Morse code. Fast fast fast. Slooooow."

After several failed attempts to restore healthy rhythm with medication, my doctor decided I should have an ablation. . . . To ablate is to burn. Yes, burn, cauterize, singe, brand. If all went well, the doctor, to use his coinage, would destroy the "misbehaving" parts of my heart.

As I was being wheeled into surgery, he asked if I had any final questions. (Not the best choice of words.)

I tried to be witty. "You're burning the interior of my heart, right?"

"Correct."

"You intend to kill the misbehaving cells, yes?"

"That is my plan."

"As long as you are in there, could you take your little blowtorch to some of my greed, selfishness, superiority, and guilt?"

He smiled and answered, "Sorry, that's out of my pay grade."

Indeed it was, but it's not out of God's. He is in the business of changing hearts.[1]

Max could have been writing *my* story! If I had only read these words several years earlier, I might have recognized my own heart "condition"—the greed, the selfishness, the superiority *I* was guilty of—and gone to the Great Physician for some much-needed surgery.

I just *thought* I was successful. I still had some hard lessons to learn. But my real Coach and the Lover of my Soul was not through with me. And like Bob, He would instruct with kindness, gentleness, and mercy.

ANGEL OF LOVE

In your union
of harmony and mutual respect,
as joint-heirs and partners,
in the kingdom of God,
I am glorified.[2]

"Angel of Forgiveness"

If you forgive those who sin against you,
your heavenly Father will forgive you.
Matthew 6:14

Chapter 4

Trouble in Paradise

I will give you a new heart, and I will put a new spirit in you.
I will take out your stony, stubborn heart
and give you a tender, responsive heart.

EZEKIEL 36:26

*Y*OU KNOW HOW IT is . . . when you have a plank in your eye, you can't see to remove the speck in your brother's eye. As I continued to rise in the real estate world, my escalating income made me the major breadwinner in our family. My head swelled right along with all of my success. I had a sense of superiority with overtones of arrogance.

Meanwhile, in my opinion, the "Mr. Right" I had married couldn't do *anything* right. Oh, nothing serious. Just those little annoyances that are a part of any marriage or long-term relationship. What a disappointment, when I had expected perfection and thought all my prayers had been answered. Hmmm. Prayer. Just *another* disappointment. . . .

We had been married ten years when Bob's company, for whom he handled acquisitions and mergers, required that he commute to Chattanooga—ninety miles away—only returning home on weekends. Since I worked on the weekends with buyers and sellers, we rarely saw each other.

With the children in the capable hands of their nanny or in school, and Bob in Chattanooga during the week, I had plenty of time to cultivate my career . . . and new friends and colleagues. While I drifted closer and closer to the brink of destruction—associating with the wrong companions and living totally in the secular world—Bob and I drifted apart, emotionally, physically and geographically.

I was all puffed up with self-importance and success. Bob was away. It was a recipe for disaster.

WHAT WENT WRONG?

One weekday morning, while Bob was in Chattanooga, I sank into my favorite chair in the den to mull over our situation. We had grown increasingly distant. I felt an emptiness in my heart, a huge vacuum where love for my husband used to be. I panicked. I didn't want to be alone and without love again. I felt like that little girl of so many years ago, standing outside a closed door, waiting to hear what my fate would be. Frightened, confused, and desperate, my life ground to a halt.

What had happened to our happiness? When had this dream, too, become a nightmare? With not a sound in the empty house, all I could hear was the hammering of my heart. In the stillness, oh so gently, a small voice whispered, *What part did you play, Jenny?*

Could *I* be the problem? The world seemed to stop turning. I froze in place. Surely not! Wasn't I the successful one?

Then began a dialogue with the little voice inside: "I've always done my best."

Except as a wife.

"I give to everyone, don't I?"

Everyone except your husband. Can you even remember the last time you were loving and affectionate with Bob?

"But I receive awards and commendations."

You might not receive My award for a Proverbs 31 woman.

That little voice was relentless!

Somewhere from deep within the catacombs of my memory, I brought up some words from Solomon's famous proverb: "Who can find a virtuous and capable wife? She is worth more than precious rubies. Her husband can trust her, and she will greatly enrich his life" (31:10-11). Those words certainly didn't describe *me* at the moment! And what about God? Where was *He* in my life?

With my family, my job, and all its perks, I was still lacking in the most important part of living—my walk with the Lord. Caught up in charting a new course for myself as a career woman, I had left Christ at the altar of that little Baptist church when I was a child. He had tapped me that day for something more, yet I had abandoned my faith for the lure of the world.

In the process, I had taken on a worldly façade—the language, the swagger, the arrogance, the partying. I was about as far from the Lord as a person can get! Suddenly, I realized I had nothing. Not peace. Not true happiness. With all my "success," I had never found the balance and stability I craved.

Something was missing. . . .

"I'VE REALLY MADE A MESS OF THINGS!"

Slowly, reality dawned: I needed God to show me the truth about myself, about my relationship with Him, about my marriage. What I thought I wanted was no longer important. Only He could see beyond the moment into the future.

I found myself on my knees, looking out my bay window toward heaven. "Lord, I've made a mess of everything!" I groaned. "I haven't been the wife Bob needs or the woman you called me to be. I'm so tired of making mistakes! Please give me a new heart and new eyes for my husband. Help me to love him as You love him."

The words of the prophet Ezekiel, from some long-ago Bible reading, came to mind: "I will give you a new heart and I will put a new spirit in you" (36:26). What a promise! Almost right away, it seemed, God performed a divine transplant, replacing my hard heart with His tender heart. I began to feel a surge of love for Bob as I realized what a gift he was, how much I valued him.

"And, Lord, I want You to direct my family, my career, my destiny. I surrender *everything* to You!"

God gives us a will of our own. He doesn't come in unless invited. That day I invited Him into every chamber of my heart. I wanted a complete housecleaning; to be honest, I really needed a makeover.

What happened next almost defies description. Through my tears, I saw shafts of brilliant light streaming through the bay window. You may not believe this, but I *know* what I saw that day, and I saw a vision of Jesus! He was wearing a robe of radiant white, His arms outstretched toward me. In my spirit, I could hear Him saying, "Come to Me, Jenny, you who are weary and heavy-laden. I will give you rest."

Oh, those life-giving words! Lying prostrate on the rug, I sobbed until there were no more tears. Waves of grace washed over my soul, cleansing every dark stain, and at last, I rested.

The windows of my soul, shuttered for years to that Light, now opened. Like a rainbow refracts the rays of sun, I felt my heart lift, filling and reflecting all the exquisite colors and characteristics of the Spirit, so alive in me. The rosy glow of Love. The golden exuberance of Joy. The soft shimmer of Peace. Patience. Kindness. Goodness. Faithfulness. Gentleness. Self-control. I barely recognized myself! I might have a distance yet to go, but this was definitely a start.

When Bob came home that weekend, he found a completely different Jenny. He took one look at me and shook his head. "What happened to you while I was gone this week?" I couldn't speak for the tears that constricted my throat, and he took me in his arms and held me. "I think I have my wife back," he murmured, burrowing his head into my hair.

I had been humbled by my Master's healing touch, and I was never the same. No more cocky attitude. No more looking for love and acceptance in all the wrong places. I had it all in Christ.

With a gentle nudge from God's sweet Holy Spirit, I copied a little poem for Bob, framed it, and placed it on his nightstand:

I'll never knowingly hurt you . . .
You'll never suffer at my hand.
I'll help you when you're down.
When you're bearing a heavy burden,
I'll get under it with you.
When you're sick, I'll pray for you.
No matter what happens in the future,
my commitment is to love you.
You don't have to love me back . . .
I love you . . . and that's that.[1]

When I feel discouraged, I read these words again to remind me of my love and commitment to this husband God has given me. Recently, after we'd had a disagreement, I noticed that he lingered to read it before leaving for work . . . with a tear on his cheek.

Several months ago, I told Bob, "Honey, I pray for you every morning. I ask that God will give you patience with me, compassion and understanding for me." I was continuing with my list of petitions, explaining how I was asking God to help him in some areas where I perceived that he needed to improve—quite selfish prayers, now that I think of it—when Bob politely interrupted.

"Well, I *have* been a faithful husband," he said in all seriousness."

Suddenly, with the force of a finger jab in the chest, the Holy Spirit convicted me. *Faithfulness! Isn't that the most important gift your husband could give you?*

I had to apologize to Bob. For nearly fifty years, unlike so many other women, I have never doubted my husband's love or fidelity to me. Our marriage has been what too many others could only dream of.

Recently I came across a story by Max Lucado in one of my favorite books on grace that moved me deeply. I'd love to share it with you:

Through a series of events, a wife learned of an act of infidelity [her husband had committed] over a decade ago. He had made the mistake of thinking it'd be better not to tell her, so he didn't. But she found out. And as you can imagine, she was deeply hurt.

Through the advice of a counselor, the couple dropped everything and went away for several days. A decision had to be made. Would they flee, fight, or forgive? So they prayed. They talked. They walked. They reflected. In this case the wife was clearly in the right. She could have left. Women have done so for lesser reasons. Or she could have stayed and made his life a living hell. Other women have done that. But she chose a different response.

On the tenth night of their trip, my friend found a card on his pillow. On the card was a printed verse: "I'd rather do nothing with you than something without you.' Beneath the verse she had written these words: *I forgive you. I love you. Let's move on.*[2]

Forgive. Love. Move on. Although infidelity has never been an issue for either of us, we have had to learn to forgive each other on less serious charges. I can't say that everything has been perfect. As Bob likes to say, "Every decade has had its challenges." But we are a work in progress, being transformed day by day into a more "perfect union." I, for one, have had a lot to learn.

FROM HIS SIDE

One lesson that I've never forgotten is something I heard when I was beginning to understand our roles as husband and wife. After forming the heavens and the earth, the moon and the stars, the plants and the animals, God was ready for the crown of His creation—man. He scooped a handful of dust from the earth and sculpted Adam, an amazing creature unlike anything He had yet made. This created being was able to communicate with Him, to walk with Him, to fellowship with Him.

But after a while, God saw that Adam needed someone more like himself—it was not good for this man to be alone. He needed a companion, a "helper." This word, *ezer* in the Hebrew language, means more than "helper," which might imply a lesser role, but "one who gives strong support." In the Bible this term is used most often to refer to military power, or even to the power of God Himself.[3]

Strangely enough, instead of creating another man from the dust of the earth, God put Adam to sleep and removed one of his ribs—the Hebrew word *tslea* means "side, flank, chamber"—to form another unique creation, "woman." When Adam woke up, he beheld his beautiful bride, delivered to him by the Creator Himself. Several Bible expositors believe that when Adam saw Eve, he was looking at a mirror opposite of himself. She offered what he lacked—both physically and spiritually—thus completing him, lending "strength."[4]

In creating Eve, God had not taken a bone from Adam's head to rule over her. Nor had He taken a bone from Adam's foot to trample on her, but a rib from his side so they could walk together, side by side, complementing and completing each other.

I love this familiar picture of the role of husbands and wives. But let me share the biblical concept from a realtor's point of view, using the analogy of a house. The job of a roof (the husband) is to cover, protect, shelter the home (the wife and children) from the elements or any threat of danger. The roof cannot stand alone; neither can a husband do his job well without the support of the strong walls (the wife's role as a "strong support"). On the other hand, if the four walls shift or move beyond the covering of the roof (such as during a marital "earthquake"), the roof will collapse and so will the walls. "If a house is divided against itself, that house cannot stand" (Mark 3:25, NIV).

In His infinite wisdom, God knew what men and women would need from one another, and He created us to fulfill those needs. What becomes a bit trickier is when our own desires or expectations exceed His.

WHAT MEN WANT FROM WOMEN (AND VICE VERSA!)

You will not believe the word that spells "love" to your man. It is not exactly what you may think. The word is R.E.S.P.E.C.T.[5] And, like the facets of a beautiful diamond, each letter represents a creative way you can "sparkle" in demonstrating your love for the one God has brought into your life. Breaking down the word, letter by letter, we can learn so much about what men really want (and need) from us:

R=RESPECT—Isn't it interesting that, when spelling out the roles of husband and wife in the Bible, God didn't mention love as the primary obligation of a wife? Of course, love is understood, isn't it? There are plenty of verses to confirm that fact:

> *Love each other.*
> JOHN 15:17

> *Love is patient and kind.*
> *Love is not jealous or boastful or proud or rude.*
> *It does not demand its own way. It is not irritable,*
> *and it keeps no record of being wronged. . . .*
> *Three things will last forever—faith, hope, and love—*
> *and the greatest of these is love.*
> 1 CORINTHIANS 13:4, 5, 13

> *Always be humble and gentle.*
> *Be patient with each other, making allowance for each other's*
> *faults because of your love.*
> EPHESIANS 4:2

Do you remember a best-selling book of several years ago titled *Men Are from Mars, Women Are from Venus?*[6] The author definitely had a point. Males and females may not be from different planets, but we *are* distinctly different.

God designed us that way on purpose.

It helps to remember we are created in our Heavenly Father's image—His powerful, protective masculine side and His tender, compassionate, feminine side. Sometimes, one or both spouses share in a blend of some or all of these characteristics. Bob and I may be a prime example.

You already know that I can be strong and determined when closing a business deal. But I am, first of all, a woman—Southern-born and bred. Some might even call me a "steel magnolia." I take delight in nurturing and encouraging others and in honoring my husband. And Bob, my tough and tender man, is fiercely protective when defending his family, but gentle as a lamb when I need a shoulder to cry on. I so respect him for his intelligence, his faithful love, and his strong support.

If I've learned anything in the past nearly fifty years with Bob, it's that he, like every other male, *needs* respect. That alone will do more for him than baking him a pecan pie or preparing one of Annabelle's fried chicken dinners. In other words, I sometimes think he'd rather *see* me live out my respect for him than hear me *say*, "I love you." Besides, I have an idea that *respect* is translated *love* in a man's vocabulary.

E=EGO—It doesn't take much to deflate the male ego, despite the fact that he may have been a star defensive end on his college football team or a rugged Marlboro man. You can wound him with something as simple as a look, a poor choice of words during a tense discussion, or even your tone of voice. In the past, I had mastered that art.

Today, I do my best to think of many creative ways to let Bob know I love and appreciate him—a little note now and then, a special candlelight meal at a table for two, an unexpected hug and kiss, a listening heart. There are a thousand little things we can do to reassure our spouses that they are front and center in our lives. And then there is . . .

S=SEX—For most men, this is the quintessential proof of love. I suppose most of them would rate it at the top of the list. What every man needs to know, however, is that the way to a woman's heart is through romance. If a woman feels loved by her husband, cherished and protected by him, she is likely to desire him physically. Because women are more romantically inclined, the man who wants an exciting sexual relationship with his wife should focus on the twenty-three other hours of the day!

To make the most of the physical dimension of marriage, a man must pursue his wife's mind as well as her body. The two are intricately connected. On the other hand, although women want to be appreciated for who they truly *are* rather than how they *look*, men are more visual. It wouldn't hurt, ladies, to forget the curlers, the cold cream, and the flannel pajamas when it's time for pillow talk! With a little unselfish thought, each can learn to please the other. The differences between us can make a fabulous and thrilling difference in the quality of one's private life.

Sex is a good idea—a God idea. Therefore, we can make it either a bit of heaven on earth; or, unfortunately for some, quite the opposite.

P=PRAISE (AND "SOFT ANSWERS")—Words of affirmation and praise are like the lyrics of a love song in our husbands' ears. "Sing" especially loudly when in public. Let others know your husband's strengths . . . and never, never betray him by sharing his weaknesses. I've noticed that when I compliment Bob in front of our friends, he brightens noticeably. In fact, he practically glows!

In your personal moments, when an argument or disagreement threatens to arise, defuse it by sweetly pointing out something wonderful he has said or done that meant a great deal to you. Solomon, one of the wisest men who ever lived, once said, "A soft answer turns away wrath" (Proverbs 15:1, NKJV).

E=ENCOURAGEMENT—One of my spiritual gifts is this one—encouragement. The word literally means "to inspire courage, hope, and spirit." It's what I love doing for other people—offering hope when there seems to be none, exhorting them to be all that they can be. It's who I am.

Once, when I came home from the office, I found Bob there ahead of me. He seemed unusually quiet and withdrawn. When I asked what was bothering him, he replied, "I've been fired. I didn't see it coming."

Unemployment—losing one's livelihood—is one of the worst things that can happen to a man. In his DNA is the divine drive to provide. God made him that way. And when the role of provider is threatened by unforeseen circumstances, it can be devastating to his masculinity.

I put my arms around Bob and assured him that everything would be fine. What he didn't need was for me to worry, too. I had been through lean times before and learned that one of the names of God is *Jehovah-Jireh*—"The Lord Will Provide." We had to take Him at His word in this situation and believe that all things would work for good. After all, we knew the Lord was the true Source of every good thing in our lives. In time, Bob's faith was rewarded when he again landed an excellent job.

C=COMMITMENT AND COMMUNICATION—

Contrary to what Hollywood and other purveyors of lies would have us believe, marriage is no fairy tale. There are times when a husband and wife may not even like each other very much. I've shared with you some of those times in our marriage.

But marriage is a covenant between the couple and God—a binding contract that goes deeper than a piece of paper. "What God has joined together let no man separate." As one pastor/counselor advised, "The word *divorce* should not even be in your vocabulary."

Sticking it out in the midst of difficulties takes communication—telling each other how you feel and why, then listening to the other side of the story. If you will take the time to understand, rather than always trying to be understood, you might be surprised what you would discover about your mate. Understanding why a person acts or reacts in the way he or she does can stir compassion and forgiveness in our hearts, and bring healing to a relationship.

T=TIME—This may be the most difficult. The world seems to be rotating more rapidly than ever, and there are endless activities and responsibilities to fill every nanosecond.

Most of them are important, even necessary. But think of time spent with your husband as an investment with the potential for rich dividends.

Here are a few tips for you: If he's a football enthusiast and you don't know a pass from a punt, learn at least five new football terms between now and the next Super Bowl game. Then watch the game with him, serving his favorite snack food. At the same time, watch his expression as you throw around your newly attained sports knowledge.

Tell him often how much you admire him for ____ (fill in the blank). Let him know that you depend on his strength, his courage, his keen insight. Tell him he's the captain of your ship (although as First Mate, you may often determine the direction of your voyage).

But whatever you decide to do, do it! The investment of your time will be worth every minute. More important than an insurance policy. More valuable than a CD at the bank. Time . . . one of your most priceless assets. Give it generously to those you love most. And that goes for every member of the family.

SUSAN'S STORY

Susan, my younger daughter, often received the crumbs of my time. But, bless her heart, she recalls her mother's finer points rather than her faults. I'll let Susan tell her story:

I'll admit it. I sometimes resented Mom's work hours. Since my love language is quality time and hers is giving, we weren't always on the same page. Still, some of my greatest treasures came from and through her. Oh, I'm not talking about things, although we are blessed to have those, too.

Don't get me wrong. She has given our family many intangibles—creating an environment of beauty and peace in our home, her passion for detail, her love for God and others. But by far one of the best was establishing the routine of morning devotions while I was young. I don't know how my parents managed it, but mornings before school included reading the Bible and praying together as a family.

We joined First Baptist Church, and we all began to soak in the masterful teaching of Charles Stanley. He had a way of communicating God's Word that made you hungry to hear more.

With those morning devotions ringing in my head and the pastor's encouragement to bring even unspoken prayer requests before the Lord, I was near tears one Wednesday night when Mom picked me up from my youth group meeting, led by Andy Stanley. For a good month, I had been thinking about a certain unspoken prayer request, wondering what I should do.

I was quiet all the way home. When she drove up in our driveway, she turned off the ignition and looked over at me with a worried glance. "What's wrong, Susan? What's on your mind? I'm your mother. You can talk to me."

"I'm afraid I don't know Jesus well enough to go to heaven!" I told her.

"Well, let's settle that right now," Mom said with that no-nonsense tone she gets when she's doing serious business.

She reached into the glove compartment of the car and pulled out a small booklet, *How to Know God*, by Billy Graham. She then shared with me how our sin separates us from a Holy God, and since we could not bridge the gap, God sent Jesus, His Son, to die on the cross to pay the price for our sin. Right there in the driveway, we prayed together, and I received the greatest gift ever—the peace of knowing Jesus as my personal Savior.

I can tell you that a great weight lifted off my heart! God is the Giver and Jesus is the Gift, of course, but Mom was the messenger, and for that, I will be forever grateful.

I [Jenny] recall that, afterward, we hurried inside to find Bob, who joined us on our knees, and together, we prayed over our daughter. It was a precious moment none of us will forget.

A MOTHER'S PRAYERS

Both of my daughters are strong believers, but I have learned that a mother's job is never done—especially in the realm of prayer. I still pray for my adult daughters and their families. I am determined that the enemy will not sabotage their beautiful lives—as he almost did mine—or steal anything more from them.

In her book, *The Power of a Praying Parent*, Stormie Omartian writes:

The battle for our children's lives is waged on our knees. When we don't pray, it's like sitting on the sidelines watching our children in a war zone getting shot at from all angles. When we *do* pray, we're in the battle alongside them, appropriating God's power on their behalf. If we also declare the Word of God in our prayers, then we wield a powerful weapon against which no enemy can prevail.[7]

I pray often for Stephanie and her family, including her husband, David, my business partner, and five grand-angels, five of my seven grandchildren. And I pray for my darling daughter, Susan, and her two precious children.

Just as when they were young, I could not be with them every moment and had to trust God with their little lives, so I will not always be around to know their every need. But God does. And He is their Father, who loves them even more than I.

WHAT THE ENEMY INTENDED FOR EVIL . . .

Having received the greatest blessing of my life—knowing Jesus as my Savior and Lord—why *wouldn't* I want to share Him with everyone I know? How grateful I am to have had the privilege of leading each one of my family members to Him, beginning with Mother, years ago, and later my children, my sister and brother, and even influencing my husband to make this decision.

Brought up as a Catholic, Bob had not been encouraged to read the Bible for himself nor did he pray with any regularity, as far as I knew. All of this was new to him. But soon after we began attending First Baptist, he joined a men's Bible study and launched his personal journey of faith.

When some friends invited us to Florida for a weekend with Bill Bright, founder of Campus Crusade for Christ, we accepted gratefully, eager to spend time with this couple in that tropical setting, as well as to hear the famous speaker.

After dinner, Bill stood up to deliver the evening message. The topic? The plan of salvation and our eternal destiny. Something about the compelling way he presented his points struck the chords of Bob's heart, and the Holy Spirit moved in a powerful way.

At the close of his message, Bill invited those in the audience who felt led to come forward and give their testimony. To my great surprise, my Bob, introvert that he was, leaned over and whispered, "Pray for me. I'm going up there and tell everyone what the last five minutes have meant to me."

I was elated! Bob had danced around that decision for some time but had never settled the matter until that moment. After that weekend, our journey together took on a new dimension with a focus and a purpose we had not known before. We would soon become partners in every sense of the word.

ANGEL OF FORGIVENESS

Stop being robbed
     of My will for a beautiful, Spirit-led home . . .
     Can you give to those you love
     what you most need yourself?
Can you be more tenderhearted,
     compassionate, forgiving, just as I am
toward you? [8]

"Angel of Faith"

When your faith remains strong through many [fiery] trials,
it will bring you much praise and glory and honor on the day
when Jesus Christ is revealed to the whole world.
1 Peter 1:7

Chapter 5

Ministry in the Marketplace

*In the desert near Mount Sinai, an angel appeared to Moses
in the flame of a burning bush. . . .
And the LORD said to him, "Take off your sandals,
for you are standing on holy ground.
I have certainly seen the oppression
of my people. . . . I have come to rescue them.
Now go, for I am sending you."*
ACTS 7:30, 33

AS A BRAND-NEW MANAGING broker, I was in the early stages of my career when my husband and I attended the annual missions conference at our church. Almost immediately, I was captivated by the speaker's compelling message—"Earthly Purpose vs. Heavenly Purpose." But his next words pierced my heart:

Don't store up treasures here on earth, where they can be eaten by moths and get rusty, and where thieves break in and steal. Store your treasures in heaven, where they will never become moth-eaten or rusty, and where they will be safe from thieves. Wherever your treasure is, there your heart and thoughts will also be.
MATTHEW 6:19-20

Convicted to the core by these verses, I almost leapt out of the pew. What followed was a whispered interchange between Bob and me.

I began with a bombshell: "Honey, I believe God is calling me to the mission field."

He was incredulous. "You mean you'd leave our children and me?"

"Of course not! You'd go with me."

There was a slight pause. "But *I* didn't get that message."

I did *not* go forward that night to surrender my life to foreign missions when the invitation was given. After that disappointing event, I sought the counsel of our senior pastor. He graciously received me in his office, ready to listen.

"Dr. Stanley, I'm confused. I was so sure I heard the Lord speak to my heart about surrendering for missions, but Bob doesn't feel the same calling. What should I do?"

He leaned back in his chair and smiled. "Jenny if the Lord were truly calling you, He would have called your husband first. When you married him, you became one— one heart, one mind, one spirit. Marriage, as you know, is a picture of our intimate relationship with God. Don't walk out from under the umbrella of protection he has given you."

I certainly didn't intend to do *that* again!

He leaned forward, locking his gaze with mine. "Besides, Jenny, look around you. People are hurting, depressed, lonely, broken. You already have a mission. Your ministry is the marketplace."

Only later, when I discovered for myself what Dr. Stanley meant did I understand that, for me, the marketplace was holy ground.

Despite my escalating career, though, I was either ready to put it on hold indefinitely or give it up altogether until my meeting with Dr. Stanley. He had spoken of ministering where you are, but he had also addressed a sensitive issue in today's society—the individual roles of husband and wife.

Dr. Stanley had cautioned me not to step out from under the protection of God or my husband. He had also given me a crash course in Marriage 101.

"God gave the husband spiritual authority to lead his family well. The wife is to use her influence to support and encourage him." It was that warning that followed me home and lingered long after our conversation was over.

I left my pastor's office, emboldened and with a new purpose: I would be more respectful of the position God had given Bob in our marriage, and I would encourage him to be all he was intended to be—just as I would often counsel my agents in years to come.

ANGEL WITHOUT WINGS

Thinking over what I had heard that day, I felt that there was only one thing to do. The children and I needed to move to Chattanooga, where Bob was working. Before he could blink, we were walking lots on Signal Mountain. I was calling around to find a builder who could build to our specifications in record time.

I wasn't particularly happy about the thought of leaving my job or the home we shared, although Bob hadn't occupied it much of the time. But that was going to change.

The thing I dreaded most was telling Mr. Denny, the man who had hired me at Northside. Mr. Denny had been my guardian angel, guiding me through the details of residential real estate, and I knew it would be upsetting to hear he would be losing one of his top agents.

While he was seated in his office one day, I tapped on the door. "Mr. Denny, may I come in? I have something to tell you."

Ever gracious, he rose from his chair and stepped around his desk. "Come in, come in. What is it, my dear? How can I help?"

"Well, Mr. Denny . . ." I began, feeling worse now that we were face to face. "I'm afraid I have some news that won't be easy for you to hear. As you know, there has been a big change in my life recently." (Mr. Denny had been one of the three people who had been instrumental in ushering me into my eternal destiny by sending me CDs of sermons and encouraging me to surrender my life to God. In the hierarchy of angels, Michael being an archangel, Mr. Denny would have been my "Michael.")

"I really hate to do this to you," I continued, fidgeting a little, "but I need to move to Chattanooga to be near my husband. Remember, you have told me that we should be reunited, and we've already found a lot and . . ."

"Oh, Mrs. Pruitt, I hope you won't do that—move, that is!" Gentleman of the old school that he was, Mr. Denny never addressed me by my first name. "You're our golden-haired child here at Northside. Don't worry, Mrs. Pruitt, I have something better in mind for you. I'll take care of everything."

"But how?"

He waved off my attempt to question him. "Just trust me. And tell Bob not to put down any money on that lot."

With that, he escorted me out of his office with a reassuring pat on my shoulder. Within forty-eight hours, he had gone to top management and requested that I be presented a job offer that neither Bob nor I could refuse. Management's offer was unprecedented. Within the month, with my husband's full approval and support, I was promoted from sales agent to Vice President and managing broker—the first female ever to hold that position at Northside.

At the same time, Bob was offered a position in the commercial real estate division that would keep him at home in Atlanta. No more commuting!

Not only that, but I was assigned a building—a small building, accommodating only about fifteen agents—but a building of my own, nonetheless. However, when Mr. Denny showed me inside, I was shocked. The place reeked of cigarette smoke, and the stained green indoor-outdoor carpeting was disgusting.

"I don't mean to complain, Mr. Denny," I said, "but I can't imagine building a new sales office under these conditions."

"You won't be creating this office in your own strength, Mrs. Pruitt. You will have your Heavenly Father with you. He has you in the palm of His hand, and He will show you how to accomplish your goals. Shall we pray about that now?"

Right then and there, we got down on our knees on that prickly green carpet, and with his hand on my shoulder, Mr. Denny prayed for me: "Father, I'm asking You to go before Mrs. Pruitt and stand behind her. I ask You to open the windows of heaven and pour out Your favor upon her. I pray that everyone who comes through these doors will receive a blessing—whether it is a contract or a word of encouragement. I pray that she will be a great influence on those you send her way. May everything that is accomplished be for Your glory. In Jesus' name, amen."

After his prayer, with tears in his eyes, Mr. Denny embraced me. "Now, you go in peace, Mrs. Pruitt. All you have to do is have faith and turn everything over to the Lord. Just use the wisdom and the gifts He has given you."

As I look back after all these years, I can see how Mr. Denny gave me the courage and confidence I needed at just the moment I needed it most. Instead of worrying and being uptight, I turned over my entire life—marriage, children, career—to the only One who could answer that prayer and show me favor. And He did just that! My marriage and home life began to flourish, and I was soon running one of the number-one offices in Northside Realty, with the smallest space and the fewest agents!

ONE BY ONE

Dr. Stanley had suggested I look around me and see the mission field close by. I had to look no further than my top agent—actually, the number-one agent in Atlanta at the time—a precious woman with sadness and desperation written all over her countenance. She had confided in me that her marriage was difficult and that she had five children to consider.

"I can't live like this, but I can't leave my husband, either." She fought back tears. "I've tried to be a good Episcopalian. . . . "

"Being good has nothing to do with it. Only God is 'good.' But He has a plan for you."

She perked up.

"I want you to come to church with me. I think you'll hear something that will help you."

She came. She heard. And by the third Sunday, when the invitation to receive Jesus as personal Savior was given, she accepted. It was my privilege to mentor her, both in the office and in her walk with the Lord. Peggie was the first of many business associates with whom I would have the honor of sharing my faith.

When they come to me asking for advice, that advice is always the same: "God wants to hear the desires of our hearts. We have not because we ask not." I encourage them to take everything to their Heavenly Father in prayer. Those who practice this simple strategy fare well.

SISTERS IN THE SPIRIT

The Lord has shown his goodness and mercy to so many He has put in my path to testify about His love—not only those surrounding me daily, but those who mean the most to me personally. Right after our mother died and my brother and sister and I were settling her estate, we realized that Mother had left some debt and the three of us would have to take care of it.

Shortly after that discovery, my sister Jackie—who was one of our agents—called. I knew that before our mother passed away, Jackie had broken up with her boyfriend and was still fragile from that sad ending. Now the rest of her world was in shambles.

"Jenny, I know we have to settle Mother's debt . . . and I'm embarrassed to tell you . . . but I have only $53 in my bank account with no listings and no closings! Would it be possible for me to borrow a little money?"

"Of course, I'll lend you some money, Jackie, you're my *sister*. But when do you think you could pay it back?"

"Well . . . I'm not sure . . ." With that, she burst into tears.

My sister was a believer, but just like me at one time, she hadn't been acting like it lately. "You don't need money, Jackie. What you need is more of Jesus. You're off the path and as lost as an Easter egg! I want you to make an appointment today with a counselor down at my church. He'll tell you what you need to do next."

That little conversation seemed to sink in, because she followed my advice and contacted Ray Holliday at First Baptist Church, where my family and I were members. He was kind enough to see her that day. Soon afterward, she joined the church and became actively involved, growing in her faith. She has not looked back.

NEW HORIZONS

Surely, life didn't get any better. Business had doubled, and we continued to set the pace for real estate sales in the Atlanta area. I had one of the top offices in the most unbelievable company in the area, great influence in the marketplace, a marriage that had rebounded and was on stable footing, and two beautiful children.

To add to my delight were the many agents who now followed my example in both business and personal decisions.

Then a call came from a dear friend who had been president of the company of a major competitor. More recently, he had moved over to an up-and-coming residential real estate agency focused on luxury homes, both resale and new construction. This company, Buckhead Brokers, was relatively small with sixty-five agents, but my friend had a big dream. He wanted to expand quickly and grow the business to 300.

My friend invited me to lunch to discuss a new opportunity. Over shrimp bisque, he rolled out a vision that inspired and excited me.

"Name your price," he said. "I will not settle for anything less than having you help me build this company."

That evening I sat down with Bob. "Honey, I think this is an opportunity we can't afford to miss." He agreed.

Now you must realize that after sixteen years at Northside Realty, my roots grew deep. I had an abiding loyalty to the organization that had given me so much. People used to say, "If you cut her open, she will bleed red and blue" (the colors of Northside's banner logo).

It would not be an easy decision. I was on my knees much of the weekend, but within seventy-two hours, I was ready to make the move.

Telling the president of Northside Realty, Johnny Isakson, about that decision was another matter. With some apprehension, I knocked on the door of his office. He rose to greet me and offered me a seat.

"What can I do for you?"

When I explained, he was shocked, to say the least. "Is there anything I could do to cause you to change your mind?"

"I'm afraid not," I replied. "I will always treasure my beginnings, but I do believe it's time to move on." We parted on the most pleasant of terms despite the awkward circumstances.

(On a side note, I hold Johnny Isakson in the highest esteem. He later moved on to become one of the most respected and admired senators ever to serve the state of Georgia. Not only is he a true statesman, but he administers his duties with a strong servant's heart in representing his constituents.)

To be honest, while I would miss my co-workers and the agents who had served under me, I was excited and eager to chart new territory.

The next day we announced my resignation at a sales meeting. I was shocked when all of the agents came to my home right away, wanting to know the details. For obvious reasons, I had not been able to take any of them into my confidence during the decision-making process. That afternoon, however, I filled them in on the company I would help to build. Within the next two weeks, eighty-five percent of those agents had followed me. I was moved beyond words.

For the next year, we were in temporary quarters while renovations were made on the building where my new company was located. When the remodel was completed, the building was a palace. At the grand opening, another surge of agents appeared, wanting to join our group. Five were from my former agency, and I could see that this would spell disaster.

Shortly after that evening, I called the managing broker of my former office. "I apologize for interrupting your day, but five of your agents have expressed an interest in moving over. When I asked them why, they gave me a list of their grievances. I think we need to talk."

He agreed to meet with me, grateful for the information I shared with him. With this heads up, he fixed the problems, greatly improving the environment of his office. If I had not put myself in his shoes, he might have been left with few realtors.

Before long, we took the new company from 65 to 350 agents and brokers, and opened two new offices.

A CAPITAL IDEA

Just when I figured I was set for the rest of my career, I received a message from Kim King, a highly respected venture capitalist in our area. He sent word that he wanted me to join him for a business lunch to discuss "a very important proposition."

Intrigued, I was also cautious as I approached the restaurant where we were to meet. What could he possibly have in mind? Everyone in town knew Kim King! He was the football legend—the quarterback from Georgia Tech—who had gone on to become equally renowned as one of Atlanta's foremost commercial real estate developers.

He got right to the point . . . even before the waiter served our water. "I don't usually do lunch, but I've been following your career, and you've made quite a name for yourself." He leaned forward, elbows on the table, regarding me thoughtfully. I didn't move a muscle, almost paralyzed to be in the presence of this industry icon. "I'm interested in helping to set you up in a business of your own."

I hesitated, weighing my words. "Thank you. I'm flattered, but I don't think I'm interested. We already have ninety agents with the best sales record in Atlanta."

He nodded but had little more to say that first meeting. We placed our orders, then ended our quick lunch with my promise to get back with him after consulting my husband. Which is exactly what I did the minute I got home!

Bob's reply: "Never close a door until you know what's on the other side."

Wise financier that he was, Bob outlined a proposal that should have sent any potential investor packing. We would expect Kim to put up all the capital, give us 51 percent ownership and total control of the company. In my mind, I added a fourth stipulation: Bob must be my partner and chief financial officer. I knew my limitations.

When I laid out the plan, including my expectations for Bob's role, expecting Kim to laugh in my face, he surprised me by saying, "Well, Jenny, I have never bought a company, merged with a company, or started a company with those restrictions . . . but for you, I'll do it. Your reputation is impeccable in this city, and, incidentally, the clincher for me was the fact that you want Bob in to manage the finances. Shows you know your strengths— and his."

Even then, I didn't shake hands on the deal, but asked for a little more time. I'd give myself the weekend to ponder and pray. It was a huge undertaking, and as confident as I was in many ways, there was still a little girl inside who wasn't quite sure of herself.

By Monday morning, I was ready to back out entirely. I put in a call to Kim, who was at that moment being interviewed on air by NBC. His assistant managed to interrupt the interview, and it was Kim himself who came on the line.

"So you've gotten cold feet," he said with a little chuckle.

"How—how did you know?"

"Oh, I've been there. But let me share something from experience: Sure, there's always some risk. But once you've made the call, you will never, ever want to be anywhere else but in control of your own destiny." He paused. "One more thing . . . I would advise you not to throw away an opportunity that may never come your way again."

I couldn't answer for another long moment. I felt as if Kim had just called the play, and I was being handed the ball with the possibility of making the winning touchdown. Pretty daunting! What if I didn't make it?

"Oh, don't worry, I'm not going to pressure you. Pray about it. Ask your pastor and your praying friends to join you. Then let me know your decision. Must run. They're expecting me back on the set."

And pray we did—Bob and I, Dr. Stanley, and a few close friends I knew to be prayer warriors. The final confirmation was Bob's sense that this was the right thing to do.

We'd do it. Together.

In October 1988, we opened Jenny Pruitt and Associates. Bob and I were business partners! It would take all the faith we could muster to embark on this new venture, but the possibilities were thrilling. The sky was the limit!

ANGEL OF FAITH

Stand up
    and take your place.
    Do the work I have called you to.
Pull down the strongholds—
    be brave, be strong!
The time is now.[1]

"Angel of Humility"

God opposes the proud but favors the humble.
James 4:6

Chapter 6

Leading from the Heart

Whoever wants to be a leader among you
must be your servant . . .
For even the Son of Man came not to be served
but to serve others and to give his life
as a ransom for many.
MATTHEW 20:26, 28

STARTING A REAL ESTATE agency would be the grandest venture we had yet undertaken. With the backing of Kim King, Bob's financial prowess, and my passion to make a difference, we would build a company of which we could all be proud. But our company would be much more than a profit-making organization.

My mind was awhirl with ideas for the new business. How to prepare our offices with luxurious, yet inviting décor that said welcome. How to market our brand of service to prospective homeowners with a distinctive flair. How to attract the best agents, professionals who would be delighted to cast their lot with us in a company of other top agents in the city. Above all, how to honor God in everything we did.

A friend once told me that he had come to believe that God hadn't just called him to be a lawyer, but to be a *Christian* lawyer—the type of lawyer Jesus would have been if He had practiced law in twenty-first century America. Now I felt He was calling me to be the kind of business leader Christ would be if He were launching a company today in Atlanta.

From the beginning, I had felt a call to reach people in the marketplace with the Good News. It was a call to ministry. In profession after profession, I see men and women more focused on their climb up the corporate ladder than their call. I believe God meant our vocations to be a platform for making an impact for Him in the world. Therefore, I made a covenant with Him that I would go anywhere to tell His story and show others how to do the same.

Here was my golden opportunity—Jenny Pruitt & Associates—with the emphasis on *Associates*. It was my vision to create a space and an environment that would draw top salespeople into our network to give homebuyers the best experience possible in locating the home of their dreams.

To do that, the key was the agent. Knowing our future agents would be our greatest assets, I would do everything within my power to help them be successful.

But how could I create an atmosphere that would cause them to want to be a part of us?

DEVELOPING A SERVANT SPIRIT

It was dear Mr. Denny who taught me the art of "servant leadership," a concept I had observed but never explored as a personal leadership style. Maybe that was because caring about others came naturally. That is, it came "naturally" after I had gotten over myself and surrendered everything to God in 1976.

Having studied the Synovus Company, chosen by *Fortune* Magazine as the best company to work for in America, I learned that people don't want to be led, but served. If leaders lead with a compassionate hand and a heart of humility, it will become an organization to be revered. This people-first philosophy—also modeled by Chick-Fil-A's founder, S. Truett Cathy, and the Ritz-Carlton—is an inverted triangle model, leading from the bottom up, with top leadership setting the tone.[1] I would make sure that tone would be mutual respect and concern for the needs of those who would decide to join us.

I stopped listening to the voices that promised instant success and put aside the books that outlined strategies for building a business. Instead, I turned to the infallible Word of God, spread out like a fine feast on a tablecloth studded with jewels. It was all there—the struggles of ordinary people, their faults and failings, and His signature stamp—His amazing grace to provide help when we need it most. And I needed it!

As I read each morning before going to the office,

nuggets of wisdom and truth sparkled from unexpected portions of Scripture. When searching for answers to some knotty problem—a verse, a line, sometimes a word or two would leap to life, assuring me that the solution would honor God and satisfy a client or agent. I soon learned this would be a lifelong journey of discovery. One never exhausts all the wonder and wisdom of the Almighty.

I was also drawn to the writings of contemporary authors whose lives and work I respected and admired—Max Lucado, Charles Stanley, Marie Chapian. Some thought or illustration from a sermon or devotional reading often buoyed me through rough waters and helped me land safely on the other side.

While we were in the beginning stages, Bob and I decided we would operate our company according to biblical principles. We asked God for His wisdom and for His hand to be on every branch and division, every decision made, and every agent and employee. We asked His help in standing against wrong and embracing what is right and good. We asked that He would help us be a light in this city and in this dark world. With that, we committed ourselves to following God's business plan—doing business His way—not following the model of some modern-day corporate guru.

The more we determined to live by these principles in the workplace, the more confident I became. Mr. Denny had often reminded me of the proverb, "As [a man] thinketh in his heart, so is he" (Proverbs 23:7, KJV). Allowing this verse to shape me—thinking I could overcome, thinking I could meet each challenge with God's power and peace, thinking I could win—I *became* a winner. I also believed if others followed my lead, they, too, could find satisfaction and success.

But another element of leadership overshadowed all the rest—something the Bible calls "the anointing" (1 John 2:27).

ANOINTED TO LEAD

Stephen, martyred for his faith in New Testament days, had it. Peter and John, two of Jesus' closest disciples, had it. Moses certainly had it—so much that when He descended from the mountain with the Ten Commandments, the Israelites could tell by his radiant countenance that He had been in the presence of the Lord.

In his book, *Leadership Promises for Your Week,* John Maxwell defines the anointing.

> Simply put, the anointing is God equipping and empowering us to succeed in what He's called us to do. . . . Anointed leadership is always characterized by these four benchmarks:
>
> 1. Charisma—Others can sense that God has truly gifted and assigned a person to fulfill a certain purpose; it seems magnetic.
>
> 2. Character—God's nature in an anointed leader is evident, and as a result, people can trust that leader.
>
> 3. Competence—An anointed leader has the ability to get the job done right. The results validate his or her calling.
>
> 4. Conviction—Anointed leaders aren't wishy-washy; they have moral and spiritual backbone and they stand up for what's right.[2]

Feeling this "calling" and believing my character and competence would prove themselves, I could move in the certainty that I was in God's will for my life. Knowing the employees and agents working with us would be watching and possibly practicing the principles that guided my decisions confirmed my belief that this was the business model we wanted to follow.

BECOMING AN ENCOURAGER

Within the first month, with the housing market doing well, our agent base swelled from a handful to thirty agents, all with impeccable résumés and experience. While the new agents were busy learning our niche of the market, contacting prospective clients, and booking listings, my job was to find ways to make their work environment a happy place and to create a climate and a culture that would ease any on-the-job stress. (I often joke that the initials *CEO* stand for *Chief Environmental Officer.*)

We had established that the décor of the office would promote beauty and peace—a reflection of everything prospective clients would anticipate finding in their new homes. With this in mind, we furnished the office with the loveliest couches, chairs, conference tables, and lamps we could find and with fine art—mostly paintings by local artists.

The spiritual dimension of the ambiance grew out of who I am, so we quickly instituted a few less conventional practices that have since become tradition. For example, conscious of our Jewish agents and of our common roots, we wanted to honor some of their religious observances. At Passover, Yom Kippur, and Hanukkah, we began to send out messages to all our people, explaining the meaning behind these festive feast days. Every Christmas, a lighted menorah is on display for eight days, alongside the Christmas decorations in every one of our offices.

In addition, all agents, clients, and employees were told about our open-door policy and were encouraged from the beginning to drop by our offices any time to discuss any topic. Nor were our cell phone numbers off limits.

A MANAGER FOR SANDY SPRINGS

Sometimes it is my joy to stand on the sidelines and champion someone else to lead from the heart. That's what happened with Nancy See.

Within sixty days of our opening, we had recruited many more people, and by our fifth year, we had opened three more offices and acquired nearly 450 agents and associates. But I was looking for a special person. I spotted her at a fundraiser for "Feed the Hungry," where some of our new agents volunteered. Even in that crowd, I saw something in Nancy that caused her to stand out.

Later she told me she was shocked when I stopped to talk with her. "The fact that you took time to single me out meant so much. You were looking at me, but you were almost looking *through* me. It felt surreal."

I remember the brief conversation I initiated with her. "Do you have your broker's license?"

"Uh, no, I don't."

"Well, get it as soon as possible. You're going to need it."

It was the Lord who led me to Nancy that day. We had been praying for the right manager for the Sandy

Springs office. I could almost see a halo over her head and knew He had great plans for her.

In that "knowing" that can only come from God, I recognized a kindred spirit in Nancy. I knew we were going to partner in ways neither of us could understand at the time. I can take people with people skills and teach them technical skills, but I can't teach people skills. That is a gift that is inherent in one's personality and character. Nancy had it.

Once she had her broker's license, she took off into the real estate stratosphere and, in due time, became a managing broker. She has since become our senior vice president and one of my dearest friends and prayer partners. When I met her, Nancy never would have believed she could have risen to such heights. Today, she not only handles delicate managerial matters with grace and poise, but she will drop everything to go with me to pray over someone's health crisis or personal problem.

Among her many attributes are critical thinking skills and sensitivity. Nancy *does* see, beyond the moment or matter at hand and into the deeper needs of the people she manages with love and compassion.

THE NECESSITY OF PRAYER

One thing I learned early in my business life: I cannot, dare not, begin a day without prayer. As much as I know about real estate, as naturally as managing and vision-casting come to me, as delightful as it is to deal with buyers, sellers, brokers, and agents, every bit of success I enjoy comes from God.

That is why I never leave home before spending at least an hour or two in His Presence, first praising Him and thanking Him for all that He means to me, then offering specific prayers and listening to anything He may want to tell me. When I reach my office, I pray again:

Lord, as I enter this workplace, I bring Your Presence with me. I speak Your peace, Your grace, and Your perfect order into the atmosphere of this office. I acknowledge Your Lordship over all that will be spoken, thought, decided, and accomplished within these walls.

I thank You for the gifts You have deposited in me, Lord. I do not take them lightly, but commit to using them responsibly and well. Give me a fresh supply of truth and beauty as I do my job. Place in my heart a spirit of thankfulness for Your goodness and Your mercy.

Anoint my creativity, my ideas, my energy so even my smallest task may bring You honor.

Lord, when I am confused, guide me. When I am weary, energize me. When I am burned out, infuse me with the Light of Your Holy Spirit.

May the work I do and the way I do it bring hope, life, and courage to all with whom I come in contact. And, Lord, even in this day's most stressful moment, may I rest in You.

In the Name of Jesus, my Savior. Amen.

But prayer doesn't stop at the door of my office. The day may hold difficult decisions, promises and commitments to keep, people to encourage. Some days are more challenging than others, but in everything we do, we seek God first. Maybe this is the reason we have been chosen to be in leadership. The Lord knows we will seize every opportunity to share Him with someone in need.

In the many requests for prayer that come our way, at least one in ten is in the area of unfaithfulness in marriage. Some agent or acquaintance will approach me, crushed and broken over a spouse who has strayed. Unfortunately, most often it is the wife who has a straying husband. I always pray that the Lord will turn his eyes and heart away from the other woman and bring him back to his first love. Just as I learned with Bob years ago, we pray for those in troubled marriages, and our advice is simply this: *Forgive. Love. Move on.*

SURVIVING . . . OR THRIVING?

Viktor Frankl was an Austrian psychologist who survived the death camp of Nazi Germany and made a significant discovery. When pursuing the question of what made it possible for some prisoners to survive those horrific conditions while others died, he concluded that the single most important factor was that survivors had a mission to perform—work left undone.[3]

This should teach us something about business. Unless everyone—employer and employee alike—shares a strong purpose and mission for the company, it may not survive.

Do you know your mission? Do you know your company's mission? I have a burning desire to help women—and men, too—stand together, become all they can be, and exert their influence for good.

Another one of my darling friends, one who shares my desire to champion others, is Camille Kesler, the first African-American woman to be elected president of the Atlanta Junior League in its nearly 100-year history.[4] While Camille is not an agent of mine, she has the same heart for those in our city who are in need, and I was honored to be on the Board during her tenure. As Atlanta Junior League is the third largest chapter in the world, with 4000 members and many time-consuming projects, Camille's burden was heavy. I was glad I could be there to pray for her during stressful times. I am even happier to call her my friend. She calls me her "amazing angel—like the angels she paints."

Camille knows this is no time for race or gender to be an issue. This is the time to follow hard after goodness, overcome evil, hang on to God's promises, and take His commands seriously. As times and seasons become more difficult to negotiate, this is the prayer I am praying. I challenge you to join me:

> Lord, what would You have me do? How can You use my company? Is there anything in my life that needs to change? I trust You to empower me to be all I should be for You. And, Lord, how may I be a part of the solution to the problems in the world around me?

It could be that His answer is as easy as A B C:

ABCS OF SERVANT LEADERSHIP

Ask for God's wisdom and understanding in every situation, and He will direct your path.

Be a shepherd to the people God puts before you—leading and protecting.

Commit your work to the Lord and your plans will succeed (Proverbs 16:3).

Don't judge a situation too quickly; sometimes there are three sides.

Err on the side of giving too much instead of too little. Be generous.

Find ways to bond with your people.

Give the benefit of the doubt to the other person.

Hope always that the best is yet to come.

Inspire others to be the best they can be by setting the example.

Join those who are committed to supporting charitable projects that will bless the poor and oppressed.

Know your people—their hopes and dreams—not just their strengths and weaknesses.

Let others see your vulnerability—it's OK to say, "I'm not sure." Don't conceal the real you. Let them see you are sometimes disappointed, sometimes hurt, sometimes righteously indignant—but always caring.

Make every effort to protect the reputation you have built; do not allow it to become diluted or distorted.

Never be afraid to admit that you're wrong; be quick to say, "I'm sorry."

Open your mind to new ideas.

Pray every day—in your private devotions, at the office, and for and with your people as opportunities arise.

Quit all forms of negative thinking.

Remain calm at all times.

Surround yourself with the best people, and then get out of the way.

Treat everyone with dignity and respect—especially when it is necessary to terminate someone.

Use your God-given gifts boldly and with confidence.

Value those things that please God rather than man.

Wise leaders stand for their convictions, no matter what the price.

Xpress appreciation for a job well done.

Your reputation will outlive you. "Choose a good reputation over great riches, being held in high esteem is better than silver or gold" (Proverbs 22:1).

Zero tolerance for workplace gossip.

I have tried to incorporate these values in our workplace philosophy, doing my best to maintain personal honor and integrity, and expecting the same from those who work with me and represent our company. Only then can we become great.

As Marie Chapian writes:

Lord, help me
To come forth like Lazarus,
Sing in prison like Paul,
Pray with wisdom like Solomon,
Dance like David,
Love like Ruth,
Be faithful like Daniel,
Have the patience of Job,
Be worthy of praise like the Proverbs 31 woman.
I want to be great . . . in Your eyes.[6]

ANGEL OF HUMILITY

If you would have the greatness
of a hero—
would you also bear the suffering?
The greatest is the least
in My kingdom,
and true greatness becomes
the lowly servant.[7]

My father, Elmore Starr Sanford (Jack), who once saved my life. I always loved his name--an ancestral name that meant so much to the family.

My mother, Luna Elizabeth Sanford. Don't know how many times I heard her say to me, "You're so smart!" She definitely had the gift of encouragement.

The Farm, circa 1940, before the large addition.
Water color by D. Kingled.

My mother and I. She loved well.

Here I am at about 14 months, inspecting some real estate.

My brother, Sandy, age 2 1/2--the year he
challenged the bull in the pasture!

At age 8, I looked pretty determined--even this early in life.

My sister, Jackie. Such a sweet expression.

A recent picture of me, with my brother and sister, taken at the 2014 annual Company Holiday Party at Cherokee Town Club in Atlanta. Mother and Daddy would be so proud of us!

Family picture, taken on our screened-in porch overlooking the serene pasture where the polo ponies graze. From left to right, first row: Zach Taylor, Susan Taylor, Sarah Boehmig, Emily Taylor, Ben Boehmig, Jack Boehmig, Stephanie Boehmig, David Boehmig, Abigail Boehmig; standing in front of the fireplace: Bob Pruitt, Jenny Pruitt, and Matthew Boehmig.

The Taylor family photo. From left to right: Zach Taylor, Susan Taylor, Louie (the family pet), and Emily Taylor.

The Boehmig family photo, taken in front of our home on a Sunday afternoon under the canopy of trees. From left to right: Ben Boehmig, Harley (the family pet), Abigail Boehmig, Matthew Boehmig, Stephanie Boehmig, David Boehmig, Sarah Boehmig, Toby (another family pet who survived Hurricane Katrina with only a broken leg!), and Jack Boehmig.

Bob and I, with our precious Shih Tzus,
Molly and Murphy.

Here we are again at our annual Company Holiday Party at
Cherokee Town Club.

Bob and I at an event on the lawn of a beautiful estate home on
Valley Road. This home was priced at $14 Million. We are pictured
in an antique Rolls Royce.

Stephanie and Susan, showering Bob with kisses!

Our amazing Shih Tzus, Molly (with the pink bows, of course!)
and Murphy.

A group of us from Jenny Pruitt & Associates who accepted
the challenge to undertake a three-day, sixty-mile walkathon
for breast cancer. We camped out for three days in a pup tent--
didn't think I had it in me!

My professional dance partner, David Spencer, and I, posing at the
Dancing Stars of Atlanta Alzheimer's event, where I raised the most
money that year--$52,000! We waltzed to "You Light Up My Life" by
Debby Boone. Much fun . . . and for a great cause!

David and I, holding our first Atlanta Fine Homes Sotheby's sign.
Little did we know then that this would be the "sign" of success--to
the tune of $2 Billion in sales in 2015!

Atlanta Fine Homes Sotheby's Management Team photo, taken at a
Manager's retreat in Laguna Nigel, California. We're pictured in front of
the yacht owned by one of our Sotheby's brokers. We choose nice places
to take our people and celebrate their success. From left to right: David
Boehmig, Lisa Johnson, Jenny Pruitt, Bill Rawlings, and Nancy See.

Here I am with Franklin Graham, CEO of the Billy Graham Association and Samaritan's Purse, at a luncheon in 2008 to celebrate the opening of the future Billy Graham Library located in Charlotte. (Photograph used by permission.)

John Brian Losh, presenting me with the Extraordinary Philanthropist Award at the Annual Luxury Real Estate Fall Conference in Atlanta, GA, in 2013. I was thrilled and surprised!

"Angel of Healing"

He forgives all my sins and heals all my diseases.
Psalm 103:3

Chapter 7

Dark Valley

Even when I walk through the darkest valley,
I will not be afraid, for you are close beside me.
Your rod and your staff protect and comfort me.
PSALM 23:4

FOR EVERY VALLEY, THERE are at least two mountains. I have danced on the summit, soared with the eagles, and breathed the rarified atmosphere of the mountaintops. There have been some challenges, of course, some rocky roads, some valleys, but they only make us stronger.

On a sunny March day in 1996 while driving to an appointment, I turned on my car stereo to listen to a praise tape. The music lifted my spirits to the clear blue skies above, and I began to praise God for His infinite blessings—strengthened family ties, the pure joy of daily work, loving friends and co-workers, but most of all, for my intimate walk with Him and the assurance of spending all eternity in His home. This wonderful life was only the beginning, a foretaste of Heaven.

I thanked Him, too, for guiding me through some of life's shadows and storms, allowing me to emerge again into the sunlight. Strangely enough, this was when God impressed on my heart that He was going to take me to a valley that was deeper and darker than any I had yet experienced.

Jenny, came the still, small voice I had come to recognize and love, *I've been with you on the mountaintops. I've been with you in the valleys. I will be with you in this one, too. Never fear, My child, I will walk with you, and when you're too weak to walk any longer, I'll carry you in My arms. But I will never leave you nor forsake you.*

Four weeks later, I experienced some alarming symptoms and consulted a doctor, who referred me to another doctor for a second opinion. Both dismissed the symptoms as harmless and told me the lab reports had come back negative. But I wasn't satisfied. Something wasn't right. I sensed the Lord stirring me: *Get one more opinion.*

* * *

Few patients occupied the plush waiting room of the specialist I would be seeing that sultry July morning. Outside, the heat index would reach triple digits by day's end. Inside the cool interior of the building, the atmosphere was hushed as others waited to hear what the future held for them.

This time, while Bob and I were seated in the privacy of the physician's office, he said gently, "I'm sorry, Mrs. Pruitt. But your tests were positive for cancer—stage 1."

Surely, one of the times in life when a person feels most vulnerable is the moment a medical professional delivers that diagnosis. With my career and my home life in full swing, I should have been unprepared for those words. The long-ago feelings of insecurity, uncertainty, and fear should have rushed back to flood my memory, block any coherent thought, and overwhelm my faith.

But I was not alone that day in the doctor's office. God had warned me and had sent His angels of mercy to buffer the report. I knew He would be faithful to His word. He wasn't about to leave me now.

HELP, LORD!

As one who has been dubbed "The Elegant Entrepreneur," I confess that I do love "pretty places," afternoon tea with friends, fine dining, and, of course, observing the social graces. I'm a Southern girl, after all, and we prefer refinement, gentility, keeping all interchanges on a higher plane. Unpleasant topics usually are not discussed. But during this season of my life, I was reduced to the reality: there is nothing elegant about cancer.

After considering the options outlined by the oncologist, Bob and I decided on an aggressive regimen of radiation and chemotherapy. But before I started treatment, my first thought was to have Dr. Stanley pray for me. In our living room, with the family gathered close, Dr. Stanley began by asking two questions: "Jenny, since unforgiveness can block healing, is there anyone in your life you need to forgive? Or is there anyone you should ask to forgive you?"

Looking around at those I loved most, I thought of past misunderstandings, frustrations, petty annoyances. Then, shifting my gaze, I looked deep into the eyes of my husband. All I could see reflected back to me were unconditional love and acceptance. I shook my head. As far as I knew, I had prayerfully settled all scores—past and present.

"One more thing—is everything right between you and the Lord?"

"Yes, Dr. Stanley. I've been walking with Him for the past twenty years, and I try to practice what I preach—at home and in my company."

"Then, let's pray." Placing his hand on my shoulder, he proceeded to present my case before the throne of God, asking Him to heal me and to be glorified in my life. It was a powerful prayer.

God's peace descended upon me—a peace words cannot describe, a calmness and serenity of spirit that the world, with all of its advanced technology and brilliant thinkers, cannot give. In that moment, God put everything into perspective: It would be fine with me if He left me here on earth for a while longer, but I was equally content to be with Him whenever he called me home.

Just before Dr. Stanley left, he mentioned that he, too, felt a calm assurance that God would use me in the days ahead.

In the months following, as I endured thirty-seven grueling radiation treatments and two rounds of chemo, I clung to His precious promise that He would not abandon me. He reminded me that He had created every cell of my body, knew my thoughts, read my heart, and had even numbered every hair on my head.

WHAT TO WEAR ON THE BATTLEFIELD

When you're fighting for your life, vanity goes out the window. By round two of the chemotherapy, I lost all my hair. Thankfully, the beauty industry has considered the fragile emotional state of female cancer patients and provided an array of wigs. I liked the wig I selected so much, I hated to part with it when my hair grew back!

On most days, though, appearance didn't matter. I was doing battle with an age-old enemy—a deadly cancer. The battle took every ounce of energy and every grain of faith I could muster. And each day, I put on—not my usual professional attire, with hair in place and makeup applied— but "the whole armor of God" (Ephesians 6:10-17):

- On my head, I placed **"the helmet of salvation."** With that piece of armor, I recalled the July day twenty years earlier when I gave Christ all access to my heart and life and accepted His sacrifice for my sins in return for eternity with Him. That exchange gave me certainty that my present circumstances as well as my future with the Lord were secure.

- Protecting my heart was the **breastplate of righteousness.** I was wearing, not my good deeds, but the everlasting rightness and justice of our God. Let's face it: Not one person on this planet is good. The Lord says so. We have a tendency to give in to the flesh, especially when the flesh is in pain. I have already spoken of my faults. It is only by God's grace that I am able to do any good deeds. While journeying through the valley of cancer, I had to rely on Him daily to keep from giving up, to continue giving to others even when I myself needed help. Thank You, Jesus!

• On my feet were not some little Italian leather number, but the sturdy **shoes of the preparation of the gospel of peace.** Wherever I went—the doctor's office, treatment rooms, or church (when I was able)—I prayed that I would walk in perfect peace, not in fear or anxiety or dread. Only then could I model how a Christ-follower faces adversity. He had promised never to leave me. It was up to me to prove I believed Him.

• In one hand I carried the **shield of faith,** a defensive weapon to repel "the fiery darts of the devil" (Ephesians 6:16). And, believe me, the devil was relentless in his attacks on my mind. *You're not going to make it, Jenny. Bob is still young and good-looking. He'll be married again the first year after you're gone.* The moment those mental assaults began, I countered them with . . .

• The **sword of the Spirit, which is the Word of God.** Our only defensive weapon, God's Word, the Bible, is powerful. Not a day went by that I did not take His prescription—His healing Word:

Don't be afraid, for I am with you.
Don't be discouraged, for I am your God.
I will strengthen you and help you. I will hold you up with
my victorious right hand.
ISAIAH 41:10

I am the LORD who heals you.
EXODUS 15:26

As for me, God will redeem my life.
He will snatch me from the power of the grave.
PSALM 49:15

You made all the delicate, inner parts of my body
and knit me together in my mother's womb.
Thank you for making me so wonderfully complex!
Your workmanship is marvelous. . . .
Every day of my life was recorded in your book.
Every moment was laid out before a single day had passed.
PSALM 139:13, 14, 16

I read these and other Scriptures over and over again during those long, dark days, praying that the Lord would spare my life. But if He chose not to, I could confidently say, like Job: "Though He slay me, yet will I trust Him" (Job 13:15, NKJV).

COMPANY BENEFITS

I had always tried to treat others as I would want to be treated and had taught my agents and managers to do the same. But it had never occurred to me that one day I would be on the receiving end, enjoying some of the love and caring I had dispensed. I guess it was their turn to comfort me.

For days and weeks, while I was undergoing treatment, I received hundreds of phone calls, cards, visits from praying friends and associates, gorgeous floral arrangements, and delicious food (which Bob enjoyed when I was too sick to eat). This outpouring of compassion from my staff and co-workers became one of the most beautiful benefits of this dark valley. As a result, we bonded even more closely.

One day, toward the end of my treatment when I was at my weakest—wondering if I would pull through—I received a call from an unexpected source. This caller was unrelated to my business, except that we had both served on the finance committee to bring a Billy Graham Crusade to Atlanta earlier that year.

Dr. Frank Harrington was a well-known Presbyterian minister in the area, but I was not his parishioner. He had heard of my bout with cancer and was calling to pray for me over the phone. That kind gesture gave my spirit the boost it needed, and I rallied. Even though I was so weak I had to be transported to radiation by wheelchair, I knew I would make it. This earthly "angel" had been dispatched just in time.

HEAVEN IS FOR REAL

When I was diagnosed, the Lord directed me to be open and transparent to protect others who might delay receiving diagnosis and treatment. Later, Katie Couric, the former news anchor, whose young husband died of cancer, must have had the same concern. Wanting to make a statement in her husband's memory, she submitted to a colonoscopy—on national television—for all the world to see.

I, too, attempted to be diligent in alerting others. I was blessed by finding my problem early, while it was Stage 1. Now, I believe in divine healing. Sometimes God chooses to heal here and now—on the spot, supernaturally—so we always pray first for His divine healing.

At other times, He uses the medical community. After praying for and with my friends, asking God to direct the process, I encourage them not to put off a trip to the doctor's office to confirm a diagnosis. To date, fifty of my friends and/or business associates have been checked for similar symptoms, and fifteen have been found to have pre-cancerous conditions. Praise God! I know of at least fifteen lives that have been saved from this disease.

Then there are those who love the Lord, pray for healing, fight bravely, yet still succumb. At those times, we trust God and hold on. The ultimate healing has come; it has just been perfected in Heaven.

At those times, the loved one is set free from pain and hindrances of all kinds to be with Jesus forever in the home He has prepared. Left behind are those who mourn, but He promises to heal their sadness, too. I love the way the Living Bible expresses this truth:

> *For I am convinced that nothing*
> *can ever separate us from his love.*
> *Death can't, and life can't. The angels won't,*
> *and all the powers of hell itself cannot keep God's love away.*
> *Our fears for today, our worries about tomorrow . . .*
> *nothing will ever be able to separate us from the love of God*
> *demonstrated by our Lord Jesus Christ when he died for us.*
> ROMANS 8:38 (TLB)

I once read the story of a couple who lost their only son at age five in a dune buggy accident. The parents were quoted as saying "There is no class or book on this planet that can prepare you to have your five-year-old son die in your arms. We know what the bottom looks like."

The writer commented, "On occasion, the world bottoms out. The dune buggy flips, the housing market crashes, and before we know it, we discover what the bottom looks like . . . but we know who is waiting there—Jesus Christ."[1]

I was at the bottom. So weak, I could barely lift my head. There was no guarantee, going into treatment, that I would survive. I just kept praying, looking for the light at the end of the tunnel. And there *is* a Light at the end of the tunnel. That Light is Jesus. Until you get there, though, you don't know if He is leading you to a cure on earth or will be escorting you through the splendor of the heavenly gates.

With cancer, you never know what a day will bring—pain, weakness, nausea, lack of appetite, no energy. This up-one-day-and-down-the-next uncertainty was particularly troubling for me because I thrive on order and routine. For one who loves people and activity, this might have been the most debilitating side effect of all.

Still, cancer is one disease where you have to walk out your faith every single day. Some days, all I could do was cry for God to hold me, carry me, comfort me. On other days, I managed to keep smiling and pass the time in the treatment room with others who were going through the same ordeal.

We were overjoyed to learn in October of that year that I was cancer-free. I would live to declare His goodness to many. That was more than nineteen years ago.

A CUP OF COLD WATER

It wasn't long after my recovery before I discovered a beautiful side effect of my illness—the ability and credibility to speak life to others who were experiencing the dark valley.

The clearest evidence I had that the Lord was assigning me to a prayer ministry was when I was invited to give a talk at a civic organization. At the end of the meeting, a lady approached me with an unusual request. "I can tell you believe in prayer. My sister is in the hospital with cluster headaches—they're worse than migraines. We've tried everything. Please come with me to the hospital and pray for her."

I agreed, not sure what I was going to say to this stranger. When I arrived, I asked the sick woman the two questions Dr. Stanley had asked me: "Is there anyone you need to forgive?" and "Is everything right between you and God?"

She thought for a moment, then replied, "Well, I can never forgive my ex-husband. . . . I've tried to be a good person . . . and my mother was a Methodist."

After reading Scripture that had blessed me when I was sick, I cried out to God for this lady. I had the privilege of leading her to the Lord and helping her forgive. Then we prayed for her healing. She walked out of the hospital the next day.

PREPARED FOR MINISTRY

Nancy and I decided that, to better prepare ourselves for this ministry, we would take a course offered by the Order of St. Luke the Physician, at a local Episcopal church. This course, open to all denominations and religious backgrounds, taught us how to pray specifically for traumatic personal issues, particularly for healing. One of the methods we learned to use is letter-writing.

When I learned of our dear friend Kim King's serious health problem, I sat down to write him a letter:

Dear Kim,

When word got to me about your diagnosis, my heart sank. I know those devastating words, *"You have cancer,"* are so hard to hear. You never know until they are said to you. That is the bad news.

The good news is that God will bear your burden. He will hold you and will carry you through the valley of cancer. You will not be able to handle this alone, but never fear, you will not have to be alone. Jesus tells us, "I will never leave you nor forsake you." If you have not already—and I'm sure you have—cry out to Him for His strength and a place of refuge. He bore my burden through thirty-seven radiation treatments and chemo. He was my strength when I had none.

The first thing I did was to have a fellow believer come to my home, gather our family together, and pray a prayer of healing. God honors the prayers of His people. Please let me know if I may do this for you.

You have been such a good friend and someone I admire so much. My prayers are lifted up for you, your family, and your doctors. Enclosed you will find a copy of a psalm that gave me much comfort during my dark hours.

God bless you and be with you, my friend.
Love, Jenny (and Bob)

Then we wrote the words to Psalm 91, which begin, "Those who live in the shelter of the Most High will find rest in the shadow of the Almighty" (v. 1) and continue with the powerful promise, "Do not be afraid of the terrors of the night, nor fear the dangers of the day. . . . For he will order his angels to protect you wherever you go" (vv. 5, 11).

A year later, having survived sports injuries on the field and recessions in the business world, Atlanta's hero, Kim King—football icon, entrepreneur of entrepreneurs, and my mentor—lost his battle with cancer. But he passed on peacefully and is at rest.

Recently, his only son, who is carrying on his father's business, approached me at a function and remarked, "You'll never know how much my father admired and respected you as a leader. He said you were one of the best investments he ever made."

As our angel investor in the formation of our first company, Kim took us under his wing, and his generosity protected us during a volatile economy. And, who knows, maybe in his Heavenly Home, he has earned real wings, after all!

ANGEL OF HEALING

When you cry out in despair
for the life of a loved one…
or for physical healing,
     do not lose heart.
Do not lose hope,
     because I hear
and I answer.[2]

"Angel of Generosity"

Honor the Lord with your wealth and the best part
of everything you produce.
Proverbs 3:9-10

Chapter 8

Man after God's Own Heart

[God] made David their king. He testified concerning him:
"I have found David son of Jesse, a man after my own heart."
ACTS 13:22 (NIV)

I WAS NOT OVERLY IMPRESSED with David Boehmig as a college student. He was tall and nice-looking—a good catch for our daughter Stephanie on most counts—but my concern was his spiritual temperature. He had a strong work ethic, keen intelligence, and obvious good taste, since he had chosen to spend whatever spare time he could manage with Stephanie. At this point, though, he was not a strong believer. This, in my opinion, trumped everything else.

If I had taken a closer look, I would have seen, even then, the fierce passion for truth in his dark brown eyes. Should have noticed the determination and tenacity that marked his long hours at a variety of after-school jobs. Don't know how I missed his kindness, gentleness, and patience when escorting our daughter on dates. A diamond in the rough, perhaps, but a diamond nonetheless.

By the time David and Stephanie married after he graduated college, he had made the decision to follow Christ fully, and I was sold on him. Through the years, my admiration has grown exponentially. He is now, like the biblical David, "a man after God's own heart."

After their marriage, our daughter happily settled into a serene lifestyle—unlike mine, but perfect for her taste—and when the children came along, she was content to stay home and create a comfortable space for them to thrive in. Meanwhile, David was building a successful banking career.

During the year after my bout with cancer, it was becoming apparent that Bob and I needed help with our bustling business. Despite residual weakness, I rarely missed a beat when I returned to work, but I was still recovering and Bob was tired. It had been his lot to keep the company going while I was undergoing treatment. He would push himself to the limit, managing both my load and his, then come home to a sick wife. One more steady hand at the wheel would be a blessing, and we sensed we knew to whom that hand belonged.

David! His degree was in finance, but he derived his inspiration from people—a rare combination. At 6' 10', he literally towered over any other candidate we might have considered. We knew he had an offer on the table to become a senior bank official, so we decided we'd better grab him before he became too expensive for our budget.

The chemistry was ideal. He fit the position perfectly. Although he had had no previous training in real estate, he was a born leader and soon exceeded our expectations. Second only to my decision to accept Bob's proposal of marriage, bringing David on board was the best decision I ever made!

A PARTNERSHIP MADE IN HEAVEN

David lost no time in becoming acquainted with our vision and our mission statement and was in agreement with the way we operated. It was as if he, like I, had been born for this business, for the roles he would be playing—first, in the mortgage division; later, as general manager, and ultimately, in 1998, as president of the company. It was as if he knew exactly what would be expected of him and how he would relate to the agents and employees. Meanwhile, Bob was delighted with more free time to do things he enjoyed, and I couldn't have been happier with my new business partner.

When David's friends heard about our collaboration, some of them reacted in disbelief. "You mean you're going to work with your *mother-in-law?*"

"Yes, I am. Jenny is astute. She's approachable, and she knows when to pause and when to press."

We sat down for an honest, hard assessment of where we stood as a company, where we hoped to be in five years, and how to achieve our goals. David and I thought alike. We dreamed alike.

In the forefront of those early conversations was a discussion of our motivation. What was the driving force that compelled us to work harder, strive for excellence, attain greater heights than in previous years, seek more highly qualified agents, and make Jenny Pruitt & Associates the best it could be? The answer was simple: Both of us loved God and other people and wanted to serve them.

When making business decisions, we sparred and debated—sometimes I played the devil's advocate; sometimes, David did. He was brilliant! One day after one of our lively discussions, I told him, "David, you can do what *I* do, but I could never do what *you* do."

THE THREE P'S OF SUCCESS

David and I have always subscribed to what we call the "Three P's of Success"—Passion, Purpose, and Prayer:

Passion—Webster defines *passion* as "a strong feeling or emotion; something that is desired intensely." I cannot imagine going to work each day to a dead-end job, something I didn't love. Certainly, there are times when we may not have a dream job. That's where endurance and patience come into play. But once we know we're in the place and position God intended for us, there is nothing better—whether that is CEO of a corporation or a stay-at-home mom. The point is to keep pressing on, whatever your season or whatever the circumstances.

Wage Pitt should have failed; instead, he succeeded. After losing ninety-seven percent of his eyesight at age five, he refused to attend a school for the blind. In public school, he kept up with the other students and played baseball and football. Remarkably, he went on to complete college and became a top-notch professor.

One of his students once asked Pitt which he thought

would be worse: blindness, deafness, or being born with no arms or legs. "None of those things!" he replied. "Lack of ambition or desire—lack of passion—that is the real handicap! If I don't teach you anything but to want to do something with your lives, this course will be a magnificent success."[1]

Our biggest enemies are not the challenges we face, but complacency, self-imposed limitations, and self-pity. We have all kinds of reasons for not doing more with our lives: If only we were thinner or taller or came from a more privileged background. But those are excuses. I could play that game, too. I've been there. But thank the Lord, I didn't stay there! And you don't have to, either.

Purpose—The worth of a life comes not in occupation, bank account, appearance, circle of friends, or even age. You are special, divinely designed with a purpose and destiny that surpasses anything the world has to offer. When God created you, He had never created a person just like you before and He never will again! There is only one you. Unique. Incomparable. Distinctive. You may not think so, but that doesn't change the truth.

He also created you to accomplish something . . . or many things . . . that only you can accomplish while you're here on earth. In fact, He choreographed the entire dance of your life—every step, every leap, every twist and turn—before you were born. No one else can fill your dancing shoes.

There is someone out there—or maybe in your home or workplace—who needs the word of forgiveness or encouragement only you can give. There is a book, a play, a symphony only you can write or compose. There is a heart to lift, work to do, possibly even a life to save that God has reserved for you alone.

Recently, I read a harrowing story that struck a resounding chord about purpose. In the parking lot of a well-known variety store, a van pulled into a handicapped parking space. Before long, the vehicle burst into flames. Several passersby noticed the fire, but thought the car was vacant until the door on the driver's side slowly opened. Unfortunately, it appeared that the driver, a disabled man, was trapped. Though several stood looking on, not a single soul ventured anywhere near to help.

Meanwhile, inside the store at the customer service desk, a cashier glanced outside, noticed the commotion in the parking lot and rushed to see if there was anything she could do. Despite the searing heat, she managed to pull the man out of the van, and dragged him to safety. Although he was engulfed in flames and was severely burned, she was miraculously unharmed. "I'm not a young person, and I have a lot of arthritis," she said, "but I didn't come away with a burn or anything. It was definitely divine intervention."[2]

I'm sure this lady might have preferred a more glamorous job—maybe in a bank or the medical profession or in real estate. But she was exactly where she was supposed to be, right on time. Did I fail to mention that she was seventy years old—past retirement age? If she had had a different job or had retired when most people are traveling or watching TV, that man might not have survived. She had a noble purpose—probably greater than anything she might have dreamed—and she fulfilled it.

Prayer—You already know prayer is the way I begin and end my day. Prayer is the lynchpin of my life. I could not, would not, dare not make a move without consulting the One Who created me for His purposes, gifted me to accomplish those purposes, and placed me where He wanted me to be, in the family and with the circumstances He decided should determine my life.

Of course, there would be decisions I was free to make that might alter His original plan—and I did, for a time. But He saved me and redirected the course of my life. For that, I am eternally grateful.

David, Nancy, and I frequently pray about matters concerning the business. We take time each morning to make our rounds. Attuned to our people, we pick up any distress signal with a pat on the back or exchange of greetings. Then, later, we may make a discreet phone call or send an email, digging a little deeper and asking if there is anything we can pray about or do. Rarely does anyone turn down an offer of help.

Often, our faith is demonstrated in some simple, behind-closed-door activity. Nothing public and pretentious. Just raw and real. This was true recently, when David walked into the office of a top agent whose son was experiencing severe anxiety attacks. Naturally, his father was concerned. "Please close the door, and let's pray," David said quietly. It was a moment of bonding that transcended normal office protocol. That the president of the company would care enough to focus on this agent's personal pain must have meant a lot.

GIVING BACK

David, Nancy, and I are neither cup-half-empty nor cup-half-full kinds of people. We love an overflowing cup, so we can give more. Since I returned to the Lord in 1976, I have had the immeasurable joy of giving back to God and to my community from the resources He has given me to steward—even in the leanest of years.

It has been our practice to give generously to a variety of worthwhile causes—everything from the Atlanta Mission to Wellspring. I could name other groups, but that would violate our desire to give anonymously on many occasions. I would, however, like to mention a few whose work impacts our community and the world.

Atlanta Mission—Dear to David's heart is the Atlanta Mission (formerly Atlanta Union Mission). As a member of the Board of Directors, David helps transform lives through Christ. With the aim of ending homelessness, the Mission provides emergency shelter, recovery programs, job attainment, and meals for over one thousand men, women, and children every day. Founded in 1938, this organization has offered hope to many thousands.[3]

David recalls a young man named Chris who inherited a small fortune when he was eighteen, then lost it all to drug addiction. When Chris ran out of money and friends, and was living on the street, he turned to Atlanta Mission. A volunteer there led him to Jesus and offered him hope. Now he wishes he had that $250,000 back so he could help others who need a hand.

Habitat for Humanity—Everyone has heard of the enterprise made famous by former President Jimmy Carter, enabling deserving, low-income people to have a home of their own. It has been our privilege at Atlanta Fine Homes to build two Habitat houses, working side by side with the occupants-to-be. One Saturday alone, twenty-three agents from our company turned out to wield hammers and saws.

I will never forget the teary-eyed face or the words of the new owner, a single mother of two, when she stepped across the threshold for the first time. "I never thought I'd have a place of my own like this. For the first time in my life, I'll feel safe."

Samaritan's Purse is a non-profit organization that follows Christ's command "to go to the aid of the poor, the sick, the suffering by providing food, medicine, and other assistance as well as the Gospel, the Good News of eternal life in the Name of Jesus Christ."[4]

When I met Samaritan's Purse president and CEO Franklin Graham, the eldest son of world-famous evangelist Billy Graham, he shared with me something of the extent of this global ministry. "We sponsor and train teams to respond quickly to international crises, offer disaster relief, send physicians and other volunteer medical personnel to needy nations under our World Medical Mission, conduct feeding programs, and build orphanages . . . among other things." Among the "other things" is Operation Christmas Child—encouraging everyone to fill shoeboxes with little toys, personal hygiene items, and lots of love, for disadvantaged children around the world.

Wellspring, founded by my good friend, Mary Frances Bowley, is fast becoming the model for rescue missions around the country. I was shocked to learn that one in four girls in the United States is sexually assaulted by age eighteen—with the average age of only eleven!—and that over 100,000 children are victimized every year.[5] My mother would have been appalled. I echo that sentiment. But more importantly, I want to do something about it.

Mary Frances recently visited Washington, D.C., to present her plan for helping rescue and rehabilitate the teens who have become innocent victims of an evil industry, with a global market grossing $32 billion per year, "second behind only the drug industry as the world's leading criminal enterprise."[6] The mission of Wellspring is to provide short-term residential care, twenty-four-hour supervision, and continuing education in life skills and job training to help these precious people become contributing members of society.

With a business to run and people to bless at home, I am not able to go everywhere and do everything I'd like to do for others. But when a disaster strikes somewhere in the world, and I hear that Samaritan's Purse is among the first responders on the ground, I can pray. I can fill some shoeboxes for Operation Christmas Child—and encourage my people to do the same. I can support my friend Mary Frances in prayer and occasionally volunteer at Wellspring. I can encourage others to put on their work clothes and sling a hammer for Habitat. And I can write a check. Maybe you can, too.

Someone has said that it is possible to tell where a person's heart is by looking at their checkbook, accountant's general ledger, or auditor's worksheet. I hope when the Lord inspects our books, He will find a heart overflowing with love for His kingdom and our fellow man—with plenty of evidence to prove it.

MENTORING MANY

I have learned the bottom line often directly reflects the amount of time and energy spent pouring into those with whom we work. One precious agent and founding partner, Rhonda Haran, who caught the vision and now uses compassionate care with her clients, once wrote a letter to encourage *me* at a pivotal time:

Dear Jenny,

As I sit down to write this letter, it occurs to me that I have never really taken the time to tell you how much you mean to me and how deeply you have impacted my life, both personally and professionally.

In my conversations with new agents, I often tell the story of how I was a brand-new agent, busy interviewing every company in town and somewhat confused about my future. Then I attended a Jenny Pruitt sales meeting, and lucky for me, you were speaking that day. I remember so vividly you talking with the agents about the Golden Rule and how important it is that we conduct our business according to this one simple philosophy.

I remember you saying that no matter what challenges we face, no matter what tough decisions we might have to make, we could always put our head on the pillow at night, knowing that we did the right thing. You went on to say that doing the right thing may not always be what is best for the bottom line . . . but that if we did the right thing and had a servant's heart, success would follow.

I have watched you live out that philosophy over and over again. How many professional women (or men) can say that over the course of ten years, there has never been a time when they questioned that their leader was someone they could count on to provide a Christ-like example in everything they do?

You have taught me so much over the years . . . but what is most important to me is that you believed in me and have seen things in me that I could not see in myself. You have inspired me to be the very best I can be and to fully leverage my God-given talents. Come to think of it, you are like a multi-level marketing program for Christ! For each person you influence, think of the lives that are touched. My focus now is to provide the same encouragement to those God brings into my life.

Love,
Rhonda

Her kind words were a blessing then—and they bless me now—but I share her letter here, particularly the last line, for one reason only: to demonstrate the ripple effect of one person's influence. It's one of my chief joys in life. You can know that joy, too, because everyone has a circle of influence. Yours may be greater than you could ever imagine.

* * *

David understands this aspect of our company's appeal. He, too, enjoys helping people achieve all that they can become amid self-doubt, adversity, or setbacks of any kind. "By providing a faith-filled workplace, we can offer the environment and spiritual resources needed to persevere in trying times—and this is reflected to the consumers."

In my opinion, David Boehmig is the definition of an angel. Strong. Powerful. Intelligent. Guardian of sacred things. Messenger of hope. When I move on to my heavenly home, our company—and all its people—will be in good hands.

Meanwhile, he would need all his God-given gifts and abilities to help me navigate the choppy waters of the next few tumultuous years.

ANGEL OF Generosity

You've chosen to help those
    who are hurting and oppressed,
and I have gone before you in
    your task. . . .
I am in you as you share
    your bread with the hungry,
as you help the helpless, clothe the naked,
    and spread My Word.[7]

"Angel of Protection"

How precious is your unfailing love, O God!
All humanity finds shelter in the shadow of your wings.
Psalm 36:7

Chapter 9

Jenny vs. Goliath

*"Have you seen the giant?" the men asked. "He comes
out each day to defy Israel. . . .
"Don't worry about this Philistine," David told Saul.
"I'll go fight him!"
"Don't be ridiculous!" Saul replied. "There's no way you
can fight this Philistine and possibly win! You're only a
boy, and he's been a man of war since his youth."
But David persisted. . . . "The Lord who rescued me
from the claws of the lion and the bear will rescue me
from this Philistine!"*
1 SAMUEL 17:25, 32-33, 37

S LONG AS I can remember, the real estate
business has been the most stable endeavor one
could undertake, although cyclical. A sure thing . . . or
as sure as anything can be in this messy world. Years of
maintaining excellence in business practices and careful
nurturing of our agents, who in turn have lavished love
and attention on their clients, had earned us a stellar
reputation in the industry.

I certainly had no intention of early retirement. After all, we were on a roll. David was president of Jenny Pruitt & Associates, and with Nancy's able assistance as Senior Vice President, we were enjoying the fruits of our labor. Despite a shaky economy, wars abroad, and political unrest in our country, people were always going to need a safe haven, a place to call home. And Jenny Pruitt & Associates was the agency where thousands of Atlantans had turned when they were looking for the location of their dreams. So I wasn't interested in giving up the profession that had brought me satisfaction, as well as a good return on my investment, allowing me to give to others.

As a visionary, however, I'm always looking ahead to the next thing God might have for me to do for Him. His Word even suggests we be alert for opportunities to "enlarge [our] territory, that [His] hand would be with [us], and that [He] would keep [us] from evil" (1 Chronicles 4:10). You may recognize this as the "Prayer of Jabez," an honorable man in the Bible who wasn't afraid to ask God for greater things. But "greater things" often come at a greater price. Before it was over, I would find out just how high the price could be.

ETERNAL OPTIMIST

It was a sultry day in downtown Chicago. Overhead, billowy clouds drifted on the breeze like huge puffs of cotton candy. Below, the streets pulsated with vibrant activity—bustling traffic, pedestrians on their way to shop or have lunch with a friend, professionals hurrying to close some important business deal. As a member of the Board of a relocation company, I was in the city to attend the semi-annual meeting of the directors.

Leaving the venue after the meeting, I fell into conversation with the CEO of a large real estate brokerage company that is affiliated with one of the world's wealthiest men.

"When are you coming to Atlanta?" I asked what might have seemed to him a random question. "We might be interested in talking to you."

The CEO raised an eyebrow, but smiled. "Oh, we normally buy much larger companies than Jenny Pruitt & Associates," he said kindly.

There was a momentary pause while I made some mental calculations. I knew that his organization acquired companies whose sales volume was in the multi-billion-dollar range, not billion-dollar enterprises like ours. We had reached that mark just the year before and were still seeing monthly gains.

"Well . . . why not do it in reverse?" I ventured. "You could purchase our moderately-sized company. In turn, that would likely attract a larger one. Just think—with two powerful brand names, the combination would make a huge impact on the Atlanta real estate market . . . and I would be willing to stay through the transition."

He shrugged and didn't pursue the matter. When my cab arrived, he ushered me into a seat and waved me off. That was the end of it, or so he thought.

Two weeks later, I placed a call to his office and was put through immediately. When he answered, I got to the point. "Have you given any thought to our little conversation after the Relo meeting in Chicago?"

"Yes, as a matter of fact, I have. We want to see your

financials, sign a confidentiality agreement . . . and, if we like what we see, we'll go from there."

Bob worked diligently and soon produced the necessary paperwork. After seeing our clean bottom line and our robust financial statement, it wasn't long before we were in active negotiations. By late summer, there was an offer on the table. One week before September 11, 2001, these negotiations broke down because of the low valuation placed on the mortgage division we owned, thus putting the deal temporarily on hold.

Then came that fateful day—9/11—when America's sense of peace and tranquility was forever shattered. The unthinkable! Terrorists violated our soil as our then unnamed enemy flew hijacked jetliners into New York City's Twin Towers. Shock waves from that horrific scene, televised live on every channel in the country, rippled from coast to coast and burrowed deeply into the heart and soul of our nation.

Yet, somehow, life had to go on.

Bob and I had made plans to attend a real estate conference in North Carolina, beginning on September 12. Still numb from the grisly scenes of the carnage, we did not cancel, but drove to Asheville in time to honor our reservation at the Grove Park Inn.

On our way to the conference venue, Bob muttered, "We should have taken that offer. The world could come to an end, and we'll never see an offer like that again."

Fortunately, my husband is married to an eternal optimist. "Oh, I wouldn't bet on it. I think we will."

That afternoon, at 2 p.m., we returned to our room to find a call waiting from the CEO I had met in Chicago.

"We're ready to accept your counter. We'll close in thirty days—cash."

Our attorneys went to work immediately. Because the buyer wanted the name of Jenny Pruitt & Associates in perpetuity, our attorney was able to work out the terms of the contract, including retaining my position with the company for five years and a non-compete clause that would expire at the end of that time, or when they were no longer paying my salary.

Perfect! This timeline would give me several years to decide whether to retire along with Bob, or restructure the remainder of my career in some other—*perhaps even more interesting*—way.

SECOND HONEYMOON

In October 2001 we closed on the sale. The offer from one of the most prestigious companies in real estate had seemed attractive. As CEO for the five years stipulated under the new management, I would be operating as usual (or so I understood), terminating in October 2006, the date we had agreed upon.

For the first two and a half years, we enjoyed a most pleasant relationship with the new owners. David now refers to that period as "a sort of honeymoon." Although he was president of Jenny Pruitt & Associates, David was never officially under contract to the new administration, and I was concerned for his future. I felt increasingly uncomfortable as an employee of the company that bore my name. We were doing business a bit differently, and it was just not a good fit. I was beginning to feel I needed to be the "captain of my own ship" once again.

For eighteen years, I had been the face of my company. My personality and code of ethics were woven throughout. With God's help, I had created the culture and the environment that had drawn many of the top agents to work with us.

As time moved on, under the new administration, I was getting the impression that my value as a business developer was not fully understood by people who should have been able to grasp what I could bring to the table. I wondered why the principals had ever wanted to buy my company and keep me on as CEO. I might have given up my name—Jenny Pruitt—but certainly not my *being*, not the essence of who I *am*.

David and I had done our best that last year. The bottom line proved it. This was the most profitable year since they had bought us out; the numbers revealed that we had been extremely hands-on. In this changing environment— not being in total control of our destiny—the only thing we could do was ponder the possibilities . . . and so we played the "What if?" game.

What if . . . we started over with a clean slate? What if . . . we were able to ensure a future for David and his family? What if . . . we could reach our full potential in the field while continuing to help others reach theirs once again?

VOICE OF AN ANGEL?

A few weeks before my contract was due to expire— in October 2006—I received a call from Sotheby's International Realty, a premier firm desiring to establish an affiliate in Atlanta. "We know that your current contract will be up in October, Mrs. Pruitt, and we're interested in sitting down with you to discuss options . . . ."

Although the proposition was tempting, something didn't feel right. A small inner voice cautioned me not to rush into anything. "Thank you, but I don't think I should discuss anything with you until I have officially left the company . . . and I have now agreed to stay on through December."

"Well . . ."—there was a long pause as the gentleman seemed to be giving serious consideration to my comment—"if you can assure us that you are indeed leaving by the first of the year, our meeting can wait. But it's only fair to tell you that we really must move on in a timely manner as we are also negotiating with another party in the area. We'll stay in touch."

I shared this news with both Bob and David that night after work. We were excited! With the reins of administration firmly back in our own hands, we could envision a future that was brighter than anything we had yet seen. Who could fault us for dreaming? Partnership with this organization would mean we could retain local ownership with a global impact since Sotheby's operates in sixty-two countries, with over 17,000 associates![1] It was a heady thought. Our marketplace ministry might be expanding exponentially! Only the Lord could do something like this.

Meanwhile, we were not at liberty to share with anyone outside the immediate family; it was much too early. I could only hope and pray that my company family would understand, if and when the time came.

So, we continued to dream—privately. Perhaps, in

the new year, we could start all over. Interesting. Our company has always been a place of second chances. Now might be the time to give *ourselves* a second chance.

KEEPING IT HONEST

Wisdom dictated that we discuss future prospects with someone who had walked that path. A good friend had sold his business and had worked out a five-year contract with the buyer. Didn't it make sense to chat with him? We thought so at the time.

Our brief discussion turned up some helpful tips. But he concluded the conversation with this recommendation: "I urge you to consult legal counsel as to what you should or should not say and do while you are still employed. Knowing you, you will want to operate under the strictest rule of law, as well as your own principles of faith."

Even at this preliminary stage, months before any discussions were held with a prospective partner, we made an appointment with our attorney. His advice was based on Georgia law governing employer/employee rights, which were quite liberal at the time, in favor of employee freedom.

Of course—and I repeat—we were not to disclose any information about any possible future projections. Nor did we share Jenny Pruitt & Associates' information outside the company. Why would I want to discredit it or bring undue negative attention to it? So we took *none* of the actions which we legally and rightfully could have taken.

Furthermore, **I believe I am the only owner with a non-compete clause that ended the day my contract ended!**

I could have begun a new company immediately upon fulfilling my contractual obligations, but negotiations with Sotheby's did not begin until March 2007, three months after I had left Jenny Pruitt & Associates.

At my retirement dinner from Jenny Pruitt & Associates, it was David's duty as president to present me with a gift on behalf of the company. The gift was not the customary watch; it was a lovely necklace that I wear proudly to this day. Kind remarks were made that night, and it was assumed by all present that I would truly retire. Maybe, for a fraction of a nanosecond, I thought so, too.

NO TIME TO RETIRE

But retirement was not for me! I lasted thirty days, restless to be back in the action. My sister, brother, and I did make a trip to discover our genealogical roots, but I wasn't overly impressed to discover that we had aristocratic blood. Besides, it's not the name, it's what you make of the name that counts. Or, as my Handbook for Life, the Bible says: "Choose a good reputation over great riches; being held in high esteem is better than silver or gold" (Proverbs 22:1).

As soon as we accepted the offer from Sotheby's to form Atlanta Fine Homes Sotheby's International, our reputation was on the line. Both with the principals of our former company and with those who did not understand that, for me, real estate is not a job, it's a calling. I relish every aspect of the business. Love the challenge. But, as I have said before, it's always the people who tug at my heartstrings. People who need to feel accepted, need to achieve, need to be encouraged. I simply couldn't retire and take up trivial, selfish pursuits when so many people still needed help to find their place in this world.

By May 1, 2007, we were open for business in a Buckhead office building, with no assurance of success. The pace of the next few days was hectic. A lot of prayer for protection and for the ability to attract the right agents. Purchasing supplies. Establishing systems. Setting up an office with both elegance and comfort in mind. In all the busyness, I was caught off guard by a shot fired across our bow.

I have always been fascinated by the story of David and Goliath in the Bible: Young shepherd boy from the Judean hill country, with nothing but a few stones and a slingshot, faces armor-clad giant . . . and wins! Little did I know when I first heard that story in the little Baptist Sunday school on the farm that, many years later, I would play a major role with a similar script and an impressive, equally intimidating cast.

HEADLINE NEWS

That bright blue-sky day in May began much like every other day, with one exception—I was not sitting behind my desk at the helm of our newly founded company, Atlanta Fine Homes. With the wheel of business in the capable hands of my staff, I was at a Garden Club auction, which I was chairing. Bob was on some lush green golf course in Florida, doing what he loves most . . . second only to spending time with our family. David and Stephanie were an ocean away in Italy, celebrating their twentieth wedding anniversary, and Nancy was at a local doctor's office with her sick husband. Later, on his death bed, this dear man would tell his wife: "One day you will be the best real estate company in the city of Atlanta."

But that day had not yet come.

Who would have suspected that by 3 that afternoon, our well-ordered world would be shaken to its foundations by a mere scrap of paper, delivered by the sheriff of Fulton County? The document? A motion for a temporary injunction, summoning me to appear in Fulton Superior Court the following morning at 9 a.m. to face charges of breaching my contract with my former company, Jenny Pruitt & Associates. My assistant called on my cell to notify me of the incident. To say I was "shocked and surprised" is an understatement!

On the way back to the office, I contemplated this unexpected situation. With my husband, my partner, and my best friend either far away or unavailable—I felt lonely and vulnerable. The mounting sensation was that I was under attack—not only professionally, but personally, in my core. As a Christian businesswoman, I was devastated.

By the next morning, when the paper hit the newsstands, I was headline news: "JENNY PRUITT & ASSOCIATES SUES JENNY PRUITT!" [3] The question implied was, "Is Jenny the plaintiff or defendant?"

Through the years, I have often been in the paper—articles, features, and photos related to various business, social, and philanthropic ventures. Fundraisers for worthy causes in our city, funerals where I have delivered the eulogy, balls and galas, picnics and parties. I was used to seeing my name in print. This time, though, it wasn't a pretty picture.

Although I had no secrets and felt my conscience was

clear, I had no idea what they might use to attack me. I had to be prepared to defend myself. I felt very much like little David facing Goliath. During my daily quiet time, I was reminded of a verse from 2 Chronicles: "O LORD, no one but you can help the powerless against the mighty! Help us, O LORD our God, for we trust in you alone" (14:11).

FACING THE GIANT

In 1995 Bob and I visited the Holy Land, walking where Jesus walked and taking in many sites of biblical historic interest. A highlight of the trip was our baptism in the Jordan River.

Another memorable stop was the Valley of Elah, forty-five minutes southwest of Jerusalem, spread between the gently rolling Judean hills. In springtime the desert floor blooms with anemones, sunflowers, and variegated lupine. Lush vineyards surround the area, and it is difficult to imagine that this beautiful spot was the site of an epic battle between a young shepherd boy and a Philistine warrior nearly three thousand years ago.[3]

According to one text, Goliath is said to have stood "six cubits and a span"—nine feet six inches tall. In all his battle gear—bronze helmet, breastplate, leg coverings, and shield carried by a servant walking in front of him— he must have resembled an armored tank! Not only that, but he was equipped with a sword, the head of which weighed at least fifteen pounds, a javelin, and a spear, any one of which could have inflicted mortal wounds.[4]

David, on the other hand, had come from the fields where he had been tending his father's sheep. Too young for the army, he had been sent to carry food to his older brothers, who had enlisted and were now hungry, suffering from lack of supplies. He was probably wearing only a short tunic and sandals—certainly not the uniform of a soldier who is facing a battle to the death. But what David lacked in bodily protection, he made up in courage and faith. Hearing the taunts of the giant and realizing that no one from King Saul's army was willing to meet the challenge, David offered to fight, despite the jeers and insults of some of the men, including his eldest brother.

When Saul offered David his own armor, David tried it on. But it was too big for him. Besides, he was not familiar with the heavy equipment and could not move about freely. Instead, he shrugged it off.

> David persisted. . . . "The Lord who rescued me from the claws of the lion and the bear will rescue me from this Philistine!" . . .

> David replied to the Philistine, "You come to me with sword, spear, and javelin, but I come to you in the name of the Lord of Heaven's Armies—the God of the armies of Israel, whom you have defied. Today the Lord will conquer you, and I will kill you and cut off your head. And then I will give the dead bodies of your men to the birds and wild animals, and the whole world will know that there is a God in Israel!

> And everyone assembled here will know that the Lord rescues his people, but not with sword and spear. This is the Lord's battle, and he will give you to us!"

1 Samuel 17:37, 45-47

David wasn't trained by army standards; he was trained by the "God of the armies of Israel." He would not resort to the conventional weapons of warfare of that day, but the everyday, handmade objects he had used while protecting his father's flocks. On many occasions, God had saved David from savage lions and bears. He now trusted the Lord to defend him from his *human* enemy.

He bent down and selected five smooth stones from the river, four of which he placed in his shepherd's pouch. He put the last stone in his slingshot, whirled it around his head, and, as he approached the giant, aimed at the only spot on his body that was visible and unprotected—the space around and above his eyes. You know the rest of the story . . . how that one stone toppled the giant and how the rest of the enemy army fled in terror.

That day in 1995, while standing near the now-dry riverbed, I had picked up five smooth stones and tucked them into my purse as a reminder of that brave young man and his faith in the One True and Living God. Several years later, the Lord would equip me for the battle of my life. This time, it would be *Jenny* and the giant.

ANGEL OF Protection

This is your finest hour.
    I have prepared you for this battle. . . .
    My Presence goes before you,
and no interior battle is too fierce
    to confront head-on, full-faced
and victorious.[5]

"Angel of Deliverance"

The Lord is my rock and my fortress and my deliverer.
Psalm 18:2, NKJV

Chapter 10

Five Smooth Stones

*This is what the Lord says: "Do not be afraid!
Don't be discouraged by this mighty army,
for the battle is not yours, but God's."*

2 Chronicles 20:15

"GOLIATH" WAS BIG AND strong and well-funded, and he was more than capable of fighting hard. Taking my cue from David, I would be defending myself with five smooth stones, that the Lord had given me for such a time as this.

FIRST SMOOTH STONE: PRAYER

Still reeling from what felt like a public attack on my character and business judgment, I did first what has become my custom since 1976. I took out the first smooth stone—and turned to the Lord in prayer. He alone could make any sense of this unforeseen development. He could read the motives of every heart. He knew what the outcome would be. I could only hope and pray for wisdom.

Of course, I called Nancy. She was the only officer in town, and she would need to be informed before the morning newspaper arrived on her doorstep. We prayed together over the phone.

Realizing that there were less than eighteen hours before I had to appear in court, I also called my attorney. While he pulled together facts and figures, Nancy and I prayed some more. I am grateful our God neither slumbers nor sleeps. He is always on call, ready to hear our petitions and bring comfort and peace. He delights in giving us the desires of our hearts if we trust in Him.

I was reminded of a beautiful picture portraying the meaning of hope, painted by an artist named Watts. In the painting, a woman is seated on a globe, representing a world that has treated her unfairly. Her eyes are bandaged, and she is not able to see the way ahead. In her hand she holds a harp, all the strings broken except one. Triumphantly, she strikes that last string, and from it, a beautiful melody fills her dark night.[1]

In the midst of a broken world, God gives us a harp with a string called *hope*. It is His invitation to reawaken faith: "Call to Me, and I will answer you and show you great and mighty things which you do not know" (Jeremiah 33:3, NKJV).

"Call to Me."—Prayer is our means of communicating with our Creator—the One who carved the mountains and the valleys, who flung the stars into the black velvet expanse of space. Then, from the dust of the earth, He formed the crown of His creation: man. Later He took woman from man's side. When

the first couple failed to obey in their Garden home, communication was broken for a time. But God provided a way back through His Son. Knowing the Son, we can know the Father's heart. And His heart is always an invitation to come closer.

"I will answer you."—Oh, how I needed to hear those words on that long and lonely night. When everyone else was far away, my Father was as near as my breath. I needed Him. Needed to know that He was listening and that He had the answers. My husband, my business partner, my best friend, even my attorney—they were only human, not knowing what the future held. But I could trust the One who had formed me in my mother's womb, the One who had given me a future and a hope. He would work it out . . . somehow.

"Great and mighty things."—Could I begin to believe that whatever tomorrow brought, God would turn it for good? This verse seemed to promise great things. God always keeps His promises. This I knew from past experience. He had brought me through the valley of cancer; now He would bring me through the Valley of Elah.

My faith, which had wavered in the shock of the motion delivered by the sheriff, began to rise. My God had never failed me. He would not fail me now. I would continue to pray. He would do the rest.

SECOND SMOOTH STONE: TRUTH

Honesty is the best policy . . . so I was taught and so I believe. History books are replete with examples of our founding fathers who told the truth. You've heard the stories. While working as a clerk in a store, Abraham Lincoln once walked three miles to return a little more than six cents that he had accidentally overcharged a customer, thus earning him the nickname "Honest Abe."[2]

At age six, George Washington hacked into his father's favorite cherry tree with his little hatchet—and, when confronted with his naughty deed, admitted it, fully expecting to be punished. Instead, young George's father exclaimed: "Run to my arms, you dearest boy . . . run to my arms. Glad am I, George, that you killed my tree, for you have paid me for it a thousand fold. Such an act of heroism in my son is worth more than a thousand trees, though blossomed with silver and their fruits of purest gold."[3]

In those days, telling the truth was "an act of heroism"—more valuable than gold. It still is, for those who cherish the godly principles upon which this country was founded. Real leaders were people of honor, integrity, and stern moral values. They still are.

As a leader who desires to follow in that tradition, I want to present the facts about an excruciatingly painful season of our lives, the unfolding saga of the lawsuit—both information that is public, as well as the more intimate issues of the heart.

I knew I had done everything in my power to fulfill my contract with the company that bought Jenny Pruitt & Associates in 2001. When their offer came, I was thinking ahead to "retirement"—sometime down the road—but not quite yet.

Scrolling through my mind were all the things I had been too busy to pursue during my most active years in real estate—writing a book, doing some speaking, consulting in my field, traveling the world with Bob. But above all, using every opportunity to continue telling others what God has done for me and that He can do the same for them. Meanwhile, I wasn't ready to throw in the towel.

THIRD SMOOTH STONE: WISDOM

Our season as a family at First Baptist Church was a time of great growth. So when I was faced with the biggest test of my professional life, I first cried out to God in anguish: "Why did You let this happen?"

After a time of reflection, I felt led to consider Charles Stanley's teaching on "Wisdom for Life's Trials"—the wisdom I needed to negotiate this maze. I had always gleaned inspiration and practical help in moments of crisis from this man of God. He had coached me through many trials. Later, I would find these notes on his In Touch web site, but he had spoken similar truth during the years I sat under his inspired teaching, and I drew from that well now:

As children of a sovereign God, we are never victims of our circumstances; our heavenly Father is in absolute control of everything that concerns us. With this in mind, trials should no longer be a source of anxiety or frustration for us because we understand they are His way of accomplishing His will in our lives.

In order to have the proper response to trials in our lives, we must always remember:

- The Lord designed each challenge to meet a specific need in our lives.

- He will cause our trials to produce positive results in us if we respond in obedience.

- Through trials, God tests our devotion and strengthens our faith.

- The hardships we face help us measure our spiritual walk with God.

- God will always help us overcome our circumstances if we trust Him. [4]

On the surface, I kept my composure so as not to alarm my associates or their clients. Inwardly, I was processing all that was taking place, trying to determine what God was teaching me through this testing time and how I might use it in the future for the benefit of others. Maybe what I had always heard was true: "Leaders are minted during the tough times."

★ ★ ★

Two "stones" remained in my arsenal. Not that I intended to launch them against my opponent. I had no desire to harm anyone, but I did have a right to protect myself and my family. It was my hope that this matter would be resolved quickly. Prolonging the lawsuit would cause greater damage to all concerned.

As I mentally replayed the scene with young David and Goliath, I recalled that David used only *one* stone in his battle with the giant. His aim was so true and his heart so pure, I am convinced that God gave him the victory that day to demonstrate His power and to elevate a young man whose heart was devoted to Him.

Actually, it was becoming clearer to me that at least two of my three smooth stones—Prayer and Wisdom—targeted my own spirit. But my motive was to bring clarity, not confusion or destruction.

As the proceedings dragged on, I learned more about the civil action against me—twelve allegations read before a superior court judge—which revolved around an alleged breach of contract.

It was time to take out the fourth smooth stone.

FOURTH SMOOTH STONE—FAITH

The next months stretched on with agonizing delays. One crushing blow followed another.

Even in the darkest days of my bout with cancer, I had clung to the hope of recovery, knowing God, my heavenly Father, was also my Great Physician. Could I not trust Him now to be my Judge?

Although I was on my knees often, my faith sometimes flickered in the winds of war. And this was *war*—a full-scale assault on all I had worked to achieve. More painful still was the fact that so many people were believing what they were reading in the paper.

Nancy recalls one humiliating incident. "It was the first meeting of the Atlanta Board of Realtors Jenny and I had attended since the newspaper had reported the pending lawsuit. As a past president, Jenny had always been held in the highest esteem by her colleagues. So you can imagine the embarrassment when we entered the room, and the board members who were seated at the long conference table, turned their heads to avoid making eye contact with us. It was dreadful! But Jenny never lost her confidence . . . or her smile!"

Nancy is kind, but behind closed doors, there were tears and anguish. These were not just fellow realtors and executives—they were personal friends. That meeting was painful. The annual meeting, held at the Cherokee Town Club on West Paces, was worse. We were seated at a far table in the back of the room. Once loved and admired, we were now shunned.

* * *

As the days and weeks crept by, I turned once again to God's Word and rediscovered the story of Abraham and Isaac. Father Abraham heard God's instruction to offer his beloved son, Isaac, as a sacrifice. It would be the ultimate test of his faith in a God he could not see, but whose voice he knew.

I could empathize with Abraham. Although I was not being asked to give up a child—as a mother and grandmother, I'm not even sure I could so quickly have agreed to *that*—Abraham didn't hesitate. The very next day, he packed up his donkey, summoned two servants, and told his son to prepare for the long trek to a distant mountain to worship. They started their journey, trusting God to provide.

I had begun my journey toward God as a child of twelve, had taken some wrong turns into a worldly lifestyle of pride and arrogance before surrendering all in 1976. Now, this business that I had felt was a ministry to glorify Him, first declared by Dr. Stanley and later confirmed by many others, must again be placed on the altar. Would the Lord take it from me this time? And would my faith be strong enough to sustain me until I knew the answer? For the question that persisted through the waiting was . . . *Why?* And all I could hear from heaven was . . . *Wait.*

SUMMARY JUDGMENT

The call came near the end of our workday. Only staff and employees—about nine of us—were present. The agents were out—either showing homes, at closings, or booking new listings. We had waited for what seemed an eternity— over a year of jumping through legal hoops and answering questions from the plaintiff's attorneys. In reality, after all was said and done, it took twenty-four hours for the final decision—rare for this judge, so I was told.

The call was made to David's office. "I have some exciting news," our attorney said. "Put me through to Jenny, and I'll tell you both at the same time."

In my office with Nancy and David, we listened as our attorney delivered the summary judgment: "All twelve of the allegations have been dismissed! The judge says they were unfounded and without merit."

Near tears, I did my best to compose myself, then pressed the intercom button to make an announcement to the rest of the staff: "Please come into my office. I have good news."

When everyone had gathered around my desk, I smiled, the first really genuine smile since the sheriff had knocked on our door. "Today the Lord has shown Himself strong. We have been exonerated."

Gasps and sighs of relief were audible.

"We've all been through a lot this year, and I want to thank you for your devotion and perseverance. But the One who truly deserves our gratitude is our great God who carried us in His arms through this ordeal."

Joining hands, that intimate circle of colleagues and loyal staff thanked God for His goodness, mercy, and protection.

Unfortunately, our competitors were not finished. Immediately, they began filing an appeal, at which point mediation was recommended. The other side hired additional counsel, and at least ten of their people showed up in the mediation room. This, too, was unsuccessful. Six months later, under threat of appeal, we agreed to a settlement to see this matter laid to rest. It was finally over.

FIFTH SMOOTH STONE—FORGIVENESS

One thing remained to be done. One stone. This one for me. I had to forgive them.

Sometimes, when I run across a powerful story that grips my heart, I just have to highlight the words and store them away to be read and reread. Most of us have heard the parable of the Prodigal Son as told in Luke 15. Rebellious son—the family "wild child—demands his inheritance early, leaves home, and spends it all in a riotous lifestyle. Only when he is out of funds and feeding pigs for a living does he decide he's had enough and heads for home.

What I had not considered was that, according to some biblical scholars, the story should really be called "The Parable of the Prodigal's Father." We get a close-up of the heart of God when a prodigal comes home.

Recently, I read a great word picture about this portrait of grace:

We can't see the face of the son; it's buried in the chest of his father. No, we can't see his face, but we can see his tattered robe and stringy hair. We can see the mud on the back of his legs . . . the empty purse on the ground. At one time the purse was full of money. But that was a dozen taverns ago. Now both the purse and the pride are depleted. The prodigal offers no gift or explanation. All he offers is the smell of pigs and a rehearsed apology: "Father, I have sinned against God and against you. I am no longer worthy to be called your son" (v. 21, NCV).

Although we can't see the boy's face in the painting, we can't miss the father's. Look at the tears glistening on the leathered cheeks, the smile shining through the silver beard. One arm holds the boy up so he won't fall, the other holds the boy close so he won't doubt.

"Hurry!" he shouts. "Bring the best clothes and put them on him. Also, put a ring on his finger and sandals on his feet . . . .[Let's] have a feast and celebrate. My son was dead, but now he is alive again! He was lost but now he is found!" (vv. 22-24).[5]

That is how our heavenly Father must feel when a prodigal returns to Him. Grateful. Generous with His grace. Overjoyed! But when *we* forgive—as the prodigal's father forgave his wayward child—the smile on God's face must outshine the sun.

I had a lot of forgiving to do. Just as my healing couldn't occur until I was able to speak forgiveness to those who had hurt me, so I realized now that we couldn't move on in our business with any degree of peace or progress until I had forgiven those who had wronged me by filing this lawsuit.

Not only that, but the negative publicity had stirred all kinds of suspicion and conjecture as to my integrity among people who had been my good friends. Those who had turned their heads and avoided greeting me when I entered a room at some function now were watching to see how I would react to our victory.

During that endless, year-long journey, I read verse after verse on forgiveness:

> *Forgive us our debts as we forgive our debtors . . . .*
> *For if you forgive men their trespasses,*
> *your heavenly Father will also forgive you.*
> *But if you do not forgive men their trespasses,*
> *neither will your Father forgive your trespasses.*
> MATTHEW 6:12, 14-15, NKJV

> *Then Peter came to Jesus and said,*
> *"Lord, how often shall my brother sin against me,*
> *and I forgive him? Up to seven times?"*

Jesus said to him, "I do not say to you, up to seven times,
but up to seventy times seven."
MATTHEW 18:21-22, NKJV

I also turned to the words of others who had faced obstacles and come through victoriously. One of these was Phil Cooke, author of *Jolt!*

When needing to forgive someone, I have learned to practice the steps he outlines in his book. "Here are four things you need to know about forgiveness," he writes:

1. Forgiveness does not make what happened to us right; it means we've made a decision not to let it control our life. By forgiving and attempting to restore the relationship, we reclaim peace of mind.

2. Forgiveness matters, even when the offending party refuses to admit guilt. When we wait for someone to admit he or she was wrong, we're placing our future in their hands. Forgiveness is, first and foremost, for our benefit, not the benefit of others. By forgiving, we're letting the pain and hurt go and moving forward.

3. Our willingness to forgive can move the other person to seek forgiveness. Or they may know what they did was wrong, but lack the courage to step forward and ask for forgiveness. When we make the first move, it opens the door and allows them to reach out and find mercy and understanding.

4. Forgiveness is easier when we accept that we all need it. When we refuse to forgive when we think

someone's offenses are greater than our own, that's pride. . . . Once we realize the depth of God's grace toward us, it's easier to extend grace to others.[6]

Yes, we could have counter-sued, but I had no heart to drag out the battle. I was tired of the negative press and eager to get on with building our new company. As a representative of the kingdom of God and my heavenly Father's daughter, I chose to forgive them. I forgave the plaintiffs. And I forgave the friends who misunderstood my motives. I can only hope that, in knowing the whole truth and hearing the other side of the story, they can now forgive me.

BACKWARD GLANCE

Stephanie had a few choice words about this difficult season long after the final judgment was rendered. "That lawsuit was a waste of time, a money drain, a distraction, a grasping at straws," she fumed to a friend. "The attacks on my mother and husband were personal attacks in an attempt to discredit them. But the two of them were as resolute as strong oak trees. They sat in that courtroom, hearing the allegations leveled against them, impugning their integrity, and did not flinch. At the office, they just continued doing what they do so well—building a company that would serve the community."

David and I had learned long ago that to preserve the tranquility of the work environment, a good leader maintains a cool head in the heat of a crisis. As he wisely observed, "It was never a matter of fighting the plaintiff who had lodged a complaint against us; it was a matter of a bad market and finding the smallest thing to celebrate. A miniscule percentage point of sales growth. A satisfied client. Regaining the confidence of our agents and homebuyers in a tough economy."

We also had learned never to react to adverse conditions around us, but to look to the only One who knows what the next turn in the road will bring. Besides, like Joseph, when you're at the bottom of a pit, where else can you look but up?

In retrospect, I can see most of the five smooth stones, along with those hard times, were intended for *me* . . . for refining me, for polishing me, and for preparing me for greater works ahead. I could only imagine what those greater works might be.

ANGEL OF Deliverance

I utterly destroy the weapon
    formed against you.
I strengthen you on your bed
    of languishing.
I lift you out of danger
    and plant you in a place
of safety and contentment.[7]

"ANGEL OF GRACE"

The LORD *God . . . gives us grace and glory. . . .*
No good thing [will He withhold] from those
who do what is right.
PSALM 84:11

Chapter 11

Atlanta Fine Homes

Commit your work to the Lord
and then your plans will succeed.
PROVERBS 16:3, TLB

*P*EOPLE OFTEN ASK, "WHY in the world did you want to start a new business? Why couldn't you just enjoy retirement? Travel with Bob. See the world. Do all the things you've never had time to do."

My answer? Why would I want to end the journey before it's over? Why would I give up the most rewarding platform the Lord has ever given me— countless opportunities to share His love with people from all walks of life? To tell them how on July 14, 1976, He met me on my knees in my den and transformed me into a new person. How, twenty years later, He walked me through the valley of cancer, and how He has sustained me through fiery trials ever since.

You see, my business *is* my ministry in the marketplace. It's the most exciting adventure of my life, and I don't want to miss a single moment! I am anticipating what He is going to do with this company and all the lives that are part of it—now and in the future.

Even with a fresh start, however, with a new U.S. president promising "change we can believe in," and with an alliance with Sotheby's International, our associates at Atlanta Fine Homes needed to help us deal with yet another obstacle. We had weathered one controversial storm. This one was of a different variety—a still slumbering economy and record numbers of people out of work. There was no question that this would dramatically impact the housing market.

IN THE EYE OF THE STORM

The year before the big lawsuit, we had all experienced, via newscasts and television, some of the deadliest natural disasters in history. In 2006, in our annual Christmas letter, I wrote,

> This past year has been challenging for many people, both here and abroad. The images of death and destruction from the catastrophic tsunami in Southeast Asia burned themselves into our consciousness. We heard horror stories, saw unbelievable photographs, contributed to relief efforts, and said prayers for those who narrowly escaped and those whose lives were taken or altered forever.
>
> But for us, here in the United States, Southeast Asia is on the other side of the world, not in our own backyard. Then the hurricanes hit home. Swirling and

lashing and laying waste to houses and businesses along our coasts, these horrendous storms delivered devastating blows. Unlike the giant tidal wave in the Indian Ocean that swept through like some fierce, angry sea serpent, lunging and then retreating, the hurricanes moved slowly and dramatically to wreak havoc in American cities.

This time the destruction was more immediate and shook us to our core. Every single life extinguished was an important one. Every single home now gone was someone's private world where dreams and dramas unfolded. But we are a resilient people. Gradually, disbelief and numbness have given way to that irrepressible spirit that characterizes us as a nation. We see the need. We rally to assist. We each offer what he or she is able to give . . . service, solace, food, clothing, shelter, money, prayers.

That has always been our focus. Looking back on that time, I recall that at the beginning of the hurricane disaster, two of our associates helped organize coverage for the WSB-TV telethon and raised over $3 million for the American Red Cross and Salvation Army. Since our company wanted to do more, we adopted five families and helped provide homes, food, clothing, and assistance in finding employment.

Had you ever thought that we are all just survivors—or victims—of life's storms?

Later that year, I lost a dear friend, Mary Malone, after her five-year battle with cancer. Before she died, she wrote to me her thoughts about life and death:

If you are looking for the path to survival, I would say to you: Go deep within yourself and find your spiritual nature. It is the essence of love. Bring it to the forefront of your life and greet each person, each challenge, each road block as an opportunity to learn more, live better, and love without conditions. Once you have done that, your life will become a marvelous adventure, and you will discover courage, freedom, and an absence of fear and regret.

Mary gained this wisdom to prepare her for the end of her life. Now, in these critical years of the Great Recession, 2008 and 2009, I would glean from her wise words to meet the next challenge. In the backwater of the legal storm that had raged around us and the threat of financial uncertainty, I could go deep and find a still place with God. With Him, there is always peace, never panic. I could find Him in the inner sanctum of His throne room . . . and see and hear things I had never known before.

GIVING IT BACK TO GOD

Meanwhile, in the Buckhead office, for the next few months it was business as usual. At least, to the casual observer. Most did not know that, while agents were busily contacting new clients, listing properties, and scheduling closings, my brother Sandy, Bob, and I were still helping to fund the company from our personal assets. There had been attorneys' fees, employee payroll, and providing all the support tools needed to help our agents accomplish their goals. How much longer could we continue to provide backing until there was a turnaround? *If* there was a turnaround.

To have as much liquidity as possible and to be wise stewards of our resources, we put both of our beach houses on the market and were considering selling our main residence—our dream home! The thought of parting with this place that had brought us so much joy was heartbreaking. This place where angels danced. This home with laughter in the walls. This serene sanctuary bathed in prayer. Was God really asking one more sacrifice of me?

Once again, I got down on my knees and surrendered. "I give it all back to you, Lord. You own this home. You own our company. You own the cattle on a thousand hills. You own my life. You bought it with Your own blood. I have no right to cling to any of it."

What I didn't know at that moment was that Bob was having his own epiphany. He, too, was praying with a passion that matched mine: "Lord, if You'll get us through this, I'll make a covenant with You: I will never again purchase another second home unless the cost is extremely modest."

After Bob prayed this prayer, within thirty days we sold *both* beach homes—the first time in well over a year that houses in this price range had moved—without losing any money at all!

By the end of the fourth quarter 2010—after almost four years of funding this venture—to our astonishment, we began to show a profit. And, in the face of unprecedented national debt and a declining economy, we have reported significant gains every quarter thereafter. Only God could have enabled our company to remain debt-free.

THE BEST OF THE BEST

Daily I am reminded that, with our transition into the 260-year-old Sotheby tradition—focus on the sale of luxury homes—I am surrounded by the best of the best. Elegant dwellings, staged to display their finest points. Opulent furnishings. Lush, manicured lawns and gardens. Gracious amenities. Oh, we don't own these properties. We merely borrow them for a time, hoping to pair each potential buyer with the ideal residence—a home for the heart. That pairing, in itself, is always a high and holy moment.

But I am not speaking merely of real estate. I am referring to the extraordinary people with whom it is my privilege to work. It's always about the *people.* Those super-charged, eager professionals who market and show these homes and handle their clients—the potential homebuyers—with grace and, yes, with love. It is they who have supported me through good times and hard times— when the market is robust and when it is in decline. When illness or hardship, misunderstandings or misperceptions, malicious gossip or blatant attacks come, these are the people I can count on to stand in the gap for me. To pray for me. To care. They have proven themselves over and over again. As I hope I have proven myself to them.

HEAVEN ON EARTH

Now that we were finally—and firmly—ensconced in our 12,000 square feet of new office space, working with simply the best agents in the business, I was curious as to what had brought them to Atlanta Fine Homes. All the negative publicity of earlier years had not deterred them, and I wondered why.

Eager to see if there was anything I could do to promote their future success, I asked a friend to interview a few of the agents after a sales meeting. Bill Rawlings, the fabulous broker/manager of the North Atlanta office, selected a representative group of some of our top agents and had them join my friend in a small conference room after the meeting. By design I was not present. I'll let my friend tell you what she learned that day:

These were highly motivated professionals who genuinely enjoyed what they were doing . . . and each other. There was an air of relaxed camaraderie, yet mutual respect as they began to share.

Lea Perez, a petite brunette go-getter, was the first to speak: "I have been with Jenny for fifteen years. First, with Jenny Pruitt & Associates, then later with Atlanta Fine Homes. I must admit, during those first few difficult months after the lawsuit, I did go elsewhere for a while. But it just wasn't the same. Once you have had the 'Jenny Pruitt treatment,' you're spoiled, and no other company will do. She and David and Bill think of every little thing to make our jobs easier—all the encouraging words, the material resources, right down to the . . . but, Charlcie," she interrupted herself, nodding toward another agent across the table, "tell your paper clip story."

To my right, an attractive blonde laughed. "Well, the company I came from didn't furnish their agents with any supplies at all. We were expected to purchase them ourselves. So I was enthralled with the idea that every office at AFH was equipped with virtually everything an agent could possibly need to perform well—from paper clips to calculators. Not only that, but the support staff is wonderful, and we need all the help we can get during a chaotic closing.

"But another thing Jenny and David do for us is to provide wonderful yard signs—wooden ones that are durable and beautifully designed. One lady, whose home was selling for a lesser figure than most of our clients, came to me one day and asked, rather apologetically, 'I know my home isn't a "fine home," but I wonder if I might use one of your wooden signs in my yard?' To which I replied, 'Of course, you may! To us, they are *all* fine homes!'"

At that point, the electricity in the room ramped up, with the other three agents' words practically tumbling over each other in their eagerness to tell *their* story. Kathy Rice, a super-sharp associate broker who recently received her Crystal Phoenix for twenty years in the Million Dollar Sales Club, added, "Although I've been in the real estate business for two decades, I came to Atlanta Fine Homes three years ago from a smaller company. But everyone here was so caring and welcoming that I felt right at home. The managers are overwhelmingly supportive. You'll never see anyone leave! Just one of the reasons is the inspirational articles sent out weekly from Jenny. So encouraging! And their generosity trickles down. This past Christmas, when I chaired a committee for a charity that provides for around a thousand families, I asked my friends at the office for contributions of time and money, and the response was phenomenal.

Everyone pitched in! It's always a blessing to be a part of this effort."

Lee Collins, from the UK, spoke next in his distinctively British accent, "I'm the new kid on the block—just been with AFH since December of 2014. But after ten years in real estate, it is here that I've reached the pinnacle of my career. This company supports and inspires us to be the very best we can be. They set high standards, then mentor us as we strive to reach those goals. You can tell by looking at a graph of last year's average agent productivity, compared to the other leading agencies in Metro Atlanta, that we far outsell the others. My wife, who was not a fan of Real Estate, says the way Atlanta Fine Homes is run has legitimized the industry in her eyes."

"And I can second that motion," said Jennifer Pino, an articulate, on-fire agent who lit up the room. "I didn't have a very high opinion of realtors, either. I was an interior designer and was quite content minding my own business until I began staging some homes for several real estate agents who worked for AFH. I was constantly impressed with their professionalism. Not long afterward, I studied for my real estate boards and got my license. In only three years, thanks to the mentoring and tutelage of Bill, Jenny, and David, I have become one of my office's top producers! No one is more surprised than I! It simply proves to me that anyone can flourish in such a supportive atmosphere. Our leaders invest quality time and resources in us, and that inspires us to give our best back to them."

Jennifer paused, the crackle of energy and passion almost palpable. "People in this office share ideas, brainstorm, help each other. We compete with each other, yes, but we're in this together. Because of this structure, we're at the top of our game."

There was another slight pause, and she straightened, her eyes locking with mine as she finished. "Recently, while in Miami at a realtors' meeting, I met a man from Sotheby's corporate office. When he asked where I worked, I told him and he remarked, 'Aren't *you* the lucky one? You're working for our poster child.' Some may think the affiliation with Sotheby's International has added a certain distinction to Atlanta Fine Homes . . . but I'm more inclined to believe it's the other way around. For the agents it's heaven on earth."

"And *I'm* inclined to believe," my friend added in reporting to me on the results of this meeting, "that their success is directly related to the position you have allowed God to hold in this company, as Founder and Chief Operating Officer."

David and I couldn't agree more!

CORE VALUES AND MISSION STATEMENT

From the inception of both our companies, a code of ethics based on biblical principles has been an integral part of our operating philosophy. While we did not have a formal mission statement in those early days, more recently we have come to appreciate the importance of writing our vision so that all our people—clients and competitors included—can know where we stand.

Core Values:
- Model the Golden Rule.
- Be a positive influence.
- Be generous and compassionate.
- Maintain integrity above all else.
- Practice good stewardship.

Purpose Statement: To serve God by serving others with the highest standard of professionalism and integrity to make a difference in the marketplace.

Mission Statement: To guide and care for our clients throughout their home-buying and selling experience by serving them as if we were doing so for our own family.

We might add a further word of encouragement to our agents and associates, taken from God's Word: *"So I run straight to the goal with purpose in every step"* (1 Corinthians 9:26, TLB). There is purpose in everything we do . . . and, as our core values and mission statement imply, that purpose is infinitely more significant than financial profit or personal success.

YOU, TOO, CAN SUCCEED

As God has blessed our company and given us divine wisdom to conduct business His way, we are reaping earthly benefits. A healthy bottom line has not necessarily been our only goal. Our chief aim has always been to use this platform for God's glory, and He has allowed us to prosper financially as well.

Some of the world's greatest people have faced the greatest challenges, but have overcome them.

Cripple a man, and you have Sir Walter Scott. Lock him in prison, and you have John Bunyan. Raise him in abject poverty, and you have Abraham Lincoln. Strike him down with paralysis, and you have Franklin Roosevelt. Have him/her born black in a society filled with racial discrimination, and you have Booker T. Washington, Marian Anderson, and George Washington Carver. Helen Keller was born blind and deaf, yet she graduated from college with highest honors and impacted the world. Margaret Thatcher, England's first and only female prime minister, lived upstairs over her father's grocery store. For a while, her childhood home had no running water and no indoor plumbing. Golda Meir, Israel's only female prime minister, was a divorced grandmother from Milwaukee.[1]

What do these people teach us? That success doesn't depend upon our circumstances, but upon overcoming our circumstances. With God on our side, we can do it. Paul, one of this world's great overcomers, wrote, "If God is for us, who can ever be against us?" (Romans 8:31).

You have read my story to this point. While I have not experienced all the problems of the people mentioned here, I have had my share. And God has carried me through. Others, with equally trying circumstances or still others, who might have appeared to have it all, did not fare as well. We could wonder why.

I think of Saul, who became the first king of Israel. When the people demanded a king like their neighbors, God gave them what they wanted, although it wasn't His original plan. What started out well for King Saul ended up as an abysmal failure when jealousy (of young David) and depression got the better of him. David's son, Solomon, who succeeded him on the throne, didn't do any better. Although Solomon prayed for wisdom to govern the people wisely, he was soon enslaved by the very power that God bestowed upon him. What followed was lust, greed, polygamy, and finally apostasy as he began to worship the gods of his heathen wives. A sorry end, indeed. And then there was Judas, one of Jesus' disciples. Someone who was close to his Master day after day, yet betrayed Him for a few pieces of silver. The ultimate betrayal! Overwhelmed by his sin, Judas killed himself. With all of heaven at his fingertips, he lost it all.

My story is not over. And if you are reading this book, neither is yours. I want to finish well, don't you? How is it that one can come to the end of life and have nothing to show for it? Perhaps these—and others like them—didn't trust God to guide their destiny. Maybe they succumbed to worldly temptations. Or maybe they failed to acknowledge Him as Lord and tried a do-it-yourself approach. In any case, they forfeited all the wonders that God had stored up for them. Nothing in this life is worth losing eternity.

Not only do I want to finish well, I want to make a difference in the lives of all those I touch—however briefly.

BECOMING A WOMAN OF INFLUENCE

It has been my good fortune—truly only by the grace of God—to be a woman who wields a certain amount of influence in my city. I want to use whatever influence I have for good. People seem to listen when I speak. They come to me for business advice and often stay to hear how to be healed or how to keep their marriages afloat or how to start a business of their own. I tell them all the answers are right there in God's Word. This Book is still as true and powerful today as the days—and years—it was inspired. This is where I get my inspiration for living a full and rewarding life, at peace with myself and those around me.

Take Proverbs 31, for example—the description of a "virtuous woman." She is the model for all who desire to be influential and impact their homes, their communities, and their world. Some have the mistaken idea that this ideal woman is shy and retiring. She steps back into the shadows, serving without a word, and is dominated by the male figures in her life. Nothing could be farther from the truth.

This woman is an excellent wife, mother, and homemaker. She is a manufacturer, importer, manager, realtor, farmer, seamstress, upholsterer, and merchant. Her strength and dignity do not come from her amazing achievements—they are a result of her reverence for God. In our society where physical appearance is highly prized, it may surprise us to learn that her appearance is never mentioned. Her real beauty comes entirely from her character.

The woman in Proverbs 31 is outstanding in many

ways. In fact, she may not be one woman at all—she may be a composite of many women. She is an inspiration for us to be all that we can be. Her fine qualities are listed in this proverb:

- hard work
- fear of God
- respect for spouse
- foresight
- encouragement
- compassion
- concern for the poor
- wisdom in handling finances

These qualities lead to success in any arena of life. They represent the kind of leadership I learned from Skipper Morrison and J.B. Denny—servant leadership.

Let's take one last look at servant leadership. How can anyone be a servant and a leader at the same time? We picture a leader out front. But I see the King of kings on his knees, washing His disciples' feet. We think of a leader as one who receives the best seat at the table, but I see Jesus cooking and serving breakfast on the seashore for some men who have been out fishing all night. We imagine a real leader seated on a throne or placed on a pedestal, but I see the perfect Son of God hanging on a cross—the innocent dying for the guilty.

Jesus said, "The greatest among you must be a servant. But those who exalt themselves will be humbled, and those who humble themselves will be exalted" (Matthew 23: 11-12).

Any success I have enjoyed has come from living my life by following the example of the Proverbs 31 woman and imitating Jesus. For all that He has done for me and for all He has allowed me to do for Him, I will forever be thankful.

ANGEL OF Grace

My dear one,
I have much MORE
to give you. I spread out
    My hands to you
to show you even greater and more
    wonderful exploits.[2]

"Angel of Destiny"

"I know the plans I have for you," says the Lord . . .
"to give you a future and a hope."
Jeremiah 29:11

Chapter 12

A Splendid Torch

Life is no brief candle to me.
It is a sort of splendid torch . . .
and I want to make it burn as brightly as possible
before handing it on to future generations.
GEORGE BERNARD SHAW

AS I WRITE, I feel a sense of urgency! There is so much to be done and so little time. My plate is full, but my heart is fuller still.

Oh, my dear friends, these dangerous days speak loudly to me of the need to stay close to our Creator. He formed me—and you—in our mothers' wombs, gave us gifts so we could be productive in this life and contribute to His eternal kingdom, then pass along the lessons we have learned on the journey. I echo George Bernard Shaw's sentiment in the quote above.

Now, seven decades after my birth, I can see that only God knew I would live through the depression of the 1930s, the war years of the '40s, the golden '50s, the protests of the '60s, the recession of the '70s, the Reagan era, the Information Age, and more recently, the early decades of this new millennium, with its rising threat of global war and pandemonium. This planet is not a pretty place right now. And you know how I love pretty places! But this is not the end of the story.

Rather than discouraging me, looking back over these years has only reassured me of God's hand on my life. The journey is not over; the tapestry is still incomplete. There is work to be done that only you and I can do. The enemy may have tried to unravel the divine plan on more than one occasion, but he can't win! He can't stop me from pursuing everything the Lord has yet for me to accomplish for Him.

I am praying—passionately—that my story will reach beyond the borders of this city and state, beyond the boundaries of time, and touch the hearts of some who may have built their lives on false hope and a distorted definition of success. The world measures success in dollars and volume and quantity. God's kingdom currency is much more valuable.

Until we know the true Source of success, we may buy into the world's view, with our attempts falling short of the goal. But when we acknowledge Him as Owner and CEO of our lives, He will take over and bring a profit to the bottom line that can never be stolen, embezzled, or squandered. True wealth. Eternal rewards. Infinite returns on investments made—such as grandchildren.

MY GRAND-ANGELS

Grandmothers have bragging rights. It's a universal law. So I hope you will indulge me as I share some little school essays written by two of my seven "grand-angels" when they were younger. Little seven-year-old Abigail, in her whimsical style, tickled me and touched my heart. Ten-year-old Sarah summed up my life in a few succinct sentences. Please understand that my granddaughters are not bragging about *me;* it's quite the other way around!

MEET NANNA PRUITT . . .

Nanna Pruitt is a woman with no excuses. She really likes to think about others, and about her company. We know she thinks carefully about things just by the way she looks. . . .

Nanna Pruitt's face is calm. You can see her light blue eyes sparkle in the sunlight. She isn't a skyscraper like my dad is, but everyone will notice her when she is in the room.

—By Abigail, age 7
(Grand-Angel #3)

MY NANNA

Everyone has someone to look up to. I look up to my Nanna. My Nanna has had a hard life. When she was young, her father died, and her mother was depressed and lost her job. Nanna being the oldest, took care of her little sister and brother. Then she got married and had my mom. The man she married was not loving and she got a divorce. A few years later she met Mr. Bob Pruitt. He was loving and loved her and my mom.

215

They got married and had my Aunt Susan. Things were looking up for many years.

My mom and dad (David Boehmig) got married, and then I was born. Then she started her own real estate company, Jenny Pruitt & Associates. When I was about 5, I rarely got to see her. She got cancer and was sick because of Kimo. We weren't allowed to see her during this time. While she was sick, she strengthened her relationship with God. Now, she is cancer-free and she is one of the biggest Christians I have met!

Even though Nanna had a hard life I think it has made her the strong person she is today.

—BY SARAH BOEMIG, AGE 10
(GRAND-ANGEL #1)

My brother Sandy would agree with Sarah's last statement. He has told me many times that, despite our difficult upbringing, he would not change a thing! "Those circumstances are what made us tough," he reminds me. "They made you a leader."

I suppose they're right. If I had not been tested at an early age, I would not have developed spiritual muscle. I would not have been able to withstand hardship—a fractured family as a child, a broken marriage, economic downturns, a life-threatening illness, a lawsuit opposite the richest man in the world, criticism, rejection, and scorn from lifelong friends. I would not have been brought to my knees earlier in my life when I strayed from the path of righteousness, causing me to cry out to God in desperation. He heard me and came to my rescue, giving me a testimony to pass on to many, many others . . . including my brother.

WOUNDED WARRIORS

Not all warriors are serving in the military. Some are fighting battles daily here on the home front—battles with illness, depression, poverty, abuse, and sometimes fighting for life itself.

I introduced my brother Sandy to the Lord through an executive conference where Adolph Koors was speaking. Sandy was so touched that he told me afterward, "I just want you to know I've decided to give my life to Christ." His walk since then has been incredible. Sandy now leads a table at an executive men's Bible study and has led many to Christ.

But there is more . . . and it happened not so long ago.

While he was piloting his small plane, the fuel pump disengaged, and Sandy crashed near Athens, Georgia. He was trapped under 1,500 pounds of steel. Four men happened to be near the field and ran to see if they could help. Seeing that Sandy was alive, one of them, a burly fellow, yelled, "I smell gas! This thing's gonna blow, but we can't leave this man here to die! While I try to lift the plane, you guys pull him out!"

God must have given the man supernatural strength to lift the wreckage that day—or maybe he was a powerful angel on assignment. After Sandy was freed, they rushed him to the emergency room of a local hospital in serious condition—punctured intestines, broken foot and hip, head fracture. It was touch and go for the first twenty-four hours.

When I reached his bedside, I knew my brother would want me to pray for him. After a prayer, I leaned over and began to quote Psalm 23 in his ear, hoping that even in his unconscious state, he could hear me. Visions of our mother on her deathbed flooded my memory.

"Yea, though I walk through the valley of the shadow of death, I will fear no evil. . . . "

There was no sign of life except for the slight rise and fall of Sandy's chest. Inhale . . . long pause . . . exhale . . . long pause . . . . I waited and prayed, half-expecting that each labored breath would be his last.

"Thou preparest a table before me in the presence of mine enemies . . ."

Death . . . the final enemy. Were these to be Sandy's final moments? No! I had prayed for too many people whose lives had been spared—even for Sandy as a two-year-old when he had gashed his arm on that broken glass in the well house. Surely . . . .

"Surely, goodness and mercy shall follow me all the days of my life."

Sandy opened his eyes and smiled at me, then closed them and sank into a deep, healing sleep. He was released from the hospital not many days later, scarred, but whole. Thank You, Lord, for yet another miracle.

Now that Sandy is well, he has a mandate. David, Nancy and I have learned that those who have received, must give. Like the three of us, my brother now will be able to testify with authority about the healing power of our God. We, too, are wounded warriors. Not to diminish the sacrifice of our brave men and women who have served our country in the military; they are true heroes.

But those of us who have been saved, healed, delivered, and set free are engaged in another kind of warfare—spiritual warfare. Our enemy is invisible but deadly. When we score a victory through the power of God, we must talk about it, preach it, and teach it!

DEAR TO ME

Beth Moore is one of my favorite Bible teachers. Whatever book of the Bible or subject she is writing about leaps to life as I read, and she takes me on a journey of the spirit I had never anticipated

Not long ago, in preparation for writing a Bible study on Paul's letters to the Thessalonians, she and a friend were ministering in Thessaloniki, Greece (the Thessalonica of the Bible). In this latest study, *Children of the Day*, she tells about Paul's great love for these people who had become so dear to him.

With that same heart, Beth writes:

My friend Chris offered a Scripture-engraved invitation for women to receive Christ as Savior. Our hearts exploded as a crowd sixty people long and several people thick pressed to the platform's edge. Before my very eyes, 'the church of the Thessalonians in God the Father and the Lord Jesus Christ' (v. 2) multiplied. The thought was almost more than I could bear.

My thoughts did somersaults from Christ's reference to those first disciples in John 17 to those original Thessalonians fewer than twenty years later and on to those newborn Christians gathered right before my eyes.[1]

My heart also does somersaults whenever I think of all those dear to me whom the Lord has allowed me to lead to Him through the years: my husband, my mother, our daughters, Sandy, Jackie, Rhonda, Peggie, Ashley, Samantha, and scores of others. We have walked together for a time here on earth, and oh, what a grand reunion we will have in Heaven, when we will never have to be separated again.

You have the same call on your life. If you have received Christ as your Savior, wouldn't you want to know that all those you love will be with you for all eternity? You can do what I did. Start at home with those you know best and then, as the Lord leads, reach out beyond that intimate circle to those He brings across your path. "If someone asks about your Christian hope, always be ready to explain it" (1 Peter 3:15). It could be someone at work, in the grocery store, on the street. Just pray, then listen for the answer. We are His hands and feet and, sometimes, even His voice.

On the other hand, it is sometimes more difficult to reach those we love the most.

LET'S CHAT . . .

The Lord knew what He was doing when "He set the solitary in families." He knew we would need each other. He also knew that family would also present some of our greatest challenges. From the notes in my *Touch Point Bible,* I read something that caused me to ponder my legacy and what would be the most valuable thing I could leave behind:

We do not know what will happen to succeeding generations. We can set up monetary trusts, but grandchildren may misuse the money. We can set aside land, but great-grandchildren may not want to live on it. We can provide education, but succeeding generations may turn their learning against family ideals.

The surest way to protect future generations is to help children and grandchildren love God, honor Him, and desire to pass that attitude on to their children and grandchildren. This one supreme legacy can then guide the way of other family legacies and give to them more profound meaning.[2]

The supreme legacy—loving and honoring God above all else. That is my primary concern. But another intangible I would like to leave my grandchildren is the capacity to think positively, to see a tiny point of light in a sea of darkness. In their teen and young adult years, when self-esteem can plunge with the chill temperature of a sometimes-hostile environment, I want to offer my grand-angels some friendly advice—from someone who's been there. I hope they'll listen.

So here are my *Ten Ways to Talk Yourself out of Feeling Sad, Bad, or Mad:*

1. Never think or speak negatively about yourself. That puts you in disagreement with God, who calls you *beloved.*

2. Meditate on your God-given strengths, not your weaknesses.

3. Don't compare yourself to anyone else. You are unique, one of a kind, an original, so don't settle for being a copy.

4. Focus on your potential, not your limitations.

5. Find out what you like to do, and strive to do it with excellence.

6. Have the courage to be different. Be a God-pleaser, not a people-pleaser.

7. Learn to handle criticism. Let it develop patience in you rather than discourage you.

8. Read God's Word to determine your worth rather than letting others do it for you.

9. Keep your shortcomings in perspective. You are still a work in progress.

10. Focus daily on your greatest source of confidence—the God who lives within you.

I pray that they—and perhaps you, if you need these words—will tuck these reminders away for a dark and rainy day.

★ ★ ★

There's so much more I would like to share with my grandchildren, although I must confess that I didn't have it all together when I was their age, either. It took life's hard knocks to catch my attention. But I would love to spare them the pain of taking the wrong road on the journey into their destiny.

Sometimes we're forced off the road by circumstances beyond our control, only to find that God—in His infinite wisdom and plan—can reroute for good what the enemy intended for evil. My grandchildren know the story of Joseph well. So do you. It's the story of the young boy, his father's favorite, who was sold into slavery by his jealous brothers. But he passed all the temptation tests— from not griping about being thrown into the pit and the prison, languishing there for many years, to resisting the advances of his master's wife when her husband was away from home.

Yes, Joseph could give great advice to my grand-angels. As Max Lucado writes,

> The lesson we learn from Joseph is surprisingly simple: *Do what pleases God.* Your co-workers want to add a trip to the gentleman's club to the evening agenda. What do you do? *Do what pleases God.* Your date invites you to conclude the evening with drinks at his apartment. How should you reply? *Do what pleases God.* Your friends hand you a joint of marijuana to smoke; your classmates show you a way to cheat; the internet provides pornography to watch—ask yourself the question: *How can I please God?* 'Do what is right in the sight of the Lord and trust the Lord' (Psalm 4:5).[3]

More than that, I want them to know that, while I pray they will stay strong and true to the Lord's purpose for their lives, whatever choices they make, I will always love them . . . fully, completely, unconditionally.

EARTH-ANGELS

If my grandchildren are my "grand-angels," then my two daughters are "earth-angels." When Stephanie and Susan were small, like all young children, they created handmade birthday cards for their father and me, get-well cards, drawings of flowers and trees and families—all works of art, in this mother's opinion. So, I framed some of them and hung them on my refrigerator or tacked them to bulletin boards, and ultimately tucked them away in a memory box. Treasures all.

More recently, I have overheard conversations where their words have poured over my heart like liquid love. It is these moments that are imprinted on my memory.

Stephanie shared with a friend:

My blessings have come in layers. Mother deposited one layer; Dad, another. Mother lives her faith and gives generously to all. Her work is just a vehicle for sharing and reaching out to others. She loves helping kids get their start in business, teaching them how to integrate their life and work. She's a go-getter, a doer, with her plate overflowing . . . .

Bob is not my biological father, but he was there when I wrecked the car. He was there when I graduated from college, and when I needed a shoulder to cry on. And he walked me down the aisle. . . .

I changed my maiden name to "Pruitt" as a surprise,

with the paperwork done on Father's Day and the court date falling on his birthday. I had always called him, "Daddy Bob." Now I call him Dad.

I hope Stephanie knows what a gift she gave both Bob and me with these affirming words. They are true treasures, more valuable than gold, more precious than diamonds or fine homes.

On the eve of a weekend retreat, Susan once wrote me a letter that blesses me to this day. In the letter, she prayed for me:

Dear Father,

What an awesome God you are. . . . Thank You for the impact that some Christ-follower had on Mom to lead her to faith in You, and that impact reached to my own life.

Lord, I ask that You would surround Mom as she sets aside this weekend for guidance on being a disciple. Lord, I pray that as the pruning process takes place, she will also know Your mercy and grace. . . . I thank You that Your Word says she can rest in You. "Those that trust in the Lord, loving kindness shall surround them. Be glad in the Lord and rejoice and shout for joy all who are upright in heart." We rejoice ahead of time for the growth that will take place in her because of her willingness to follow You.

In Jesus' Name, amen.

Mom, enjoy the walk and discover the Treasure!
I love you,
Susan

For all that I would like to leave to my darling daughters, they have given me even more. Seeing their godly maturity and wisdom as young adults, I am overwhelmed. The apostle John said it best: "I could have no greater joy than to hear that my children are following the truth" (3 John 1:4).

HEIR APPARENT

In one of our early-morning management meetings— "slaying the dragons," as David likes to call it—he eyed me wistfully. "Jenny, when you have moved on to your mansion in Glory, it just won't be the same around here."

I responded with a little chuckle. "Oh, I don't know. The two of us are so much alike, I suspect that very little will change."

Lest the moment become too morbid, I added, "You'll be in charge, of course, but I'll be in that 'great cloud of witnesses' mentioned in Hebrews. Or maybe God will give me wings . . . and I'll be hovering over you, delighting in every move you make. You may even hear the voice of an 'angel' suggesting a few tweaks to your plan."

After that little interchange, we quickly moved on to a discussion of the day's agenda. But it left me pondering the future. I don't think the Lord is through with me yet, and being the visionary I am, I like to think ahead. . . .

THAT FAIR CITY

We have covered many miles on this journey together, you and I. I pray that you have received encouragement for your walk. Some of you are dear friends; some are friends I have yet to meet. But all of us will one day arrive at our destination. At different times, no doubt. In different ways. Still we will come to the end of our journey.

As I contemplate that time—in the distant future, I hope—I think of the place Jesus is preparing for me. Wouldn't you love to get a peek at your new home? I know *I* would. I'm sure it will be the finest of all, the ultimate Dream House, constructed of materials that are not of this world—jasper and sardius and beryl and sardonyx. Not one of the top listings in our catalog at Atlanta Fine Homes or Sotheby's International could compare with it.

There are no earth-words to describe the incomparable beauty we will behold with our perfect vision. Delight upon delight will greet our heightened senses. Even the prophet John, when writing the Revelation and attempting to describe the heavenly vision he was allowed to see, could only say that the streets were paved with gold so pure, they *seemed* as transparent as glass! And there was a river flowing with water *like* crystal!

But here my vivid imagination takes over. What about the aroma from the celestial gardens—wouldn't that scent be the essence of heaven? Every delicate and fiery fragrance, blended to pure perfection, and rising from a visual feast of flowers and other green and growing things. I know there will be music—music such as we have never known on this planet. Music of the spheres. Notes of bliss. Crescendos of praise, encircling our heads and piercing our hearts with splendor. I'm sure we will experience sheer ecstasy in the presence of the One we will be worshiping for all eternity. I wonder if even our glorified bodies can begin to contain the joy and wonder of it all?!

Surrounding the city where our new homes will be located are twelve gates, each fashioned of a single pearl. Inside one of the heavenly gates, Mother will be waiting to welcome me, and there will be a grand reunion. I will see Ashley and Peggie again and all those other dear ones who have gone before. Abraham and Sarah, Joseph, Esther, Ruth, Mary, and David—the giant-killer, the sweet shepherd of Israel, the warrior King! And the angels! Oh, the angels! Cherubim and seraphim! Michael and Gabriel . . . and some I may recognize from glimpses I have had here on earth, dispatched to help me through some stark moment of trial or terror.

But I won't be satisfied until I see *Him*. The One who rescued me long ago. The One who holds my heart in His hands. The One who died for me and now lives eternally in this Fair City. I can see it now: His arms outstretched, His countenance radiant with light that dispels all darkness.

I can hear His sweet voice, saying again: "Come to Me, Jenny . . . you who are weary and heavy-laden . . . and I will give you rest." This time, though, it will be forever . . .

And then, with the sound of many rushing waters and with unparalleled love and tenderness, I will hear Him say at last the words I have longed to hear: "Well done, Jenny, My good and faithful servant."

Angel of Destiny

I am your health, your energy: I bring you
    to a grand finish that is not the end,
not a place where you collapse,
    emptied out, done.
It is a place where you
    allow Me freely
to live through you,
    consummating My purposes
and your destiny.[4]

Epilogue

I WOULD BE REMISS IF I didn't pause to consider all the work that is yet to be done. In addition to those we have attempted to serve—both in my business and among the needy of our community—I wonder if I have done everything I could have done.

When asked to pray at an Atlanta Rotary Club Prayer Breakfast, I had considered this matter. In reflecting on my life, I had asked myself: *When I stand before the Lord one day to give account of my life, what will I hear Him say? What will you hear?*

Where were you when my little children were hungry and homeless in the streets of your city?

Where were you when the least, the left-out, and the lost needed to hear My words through you?

Where were you when crime and violence prevailed? And when the abandoned children needed role models to learn right from wrong? And when My people needed education so ignorance and hopelessness would not abound? Didn't you remember that I taught you that what you do for the least of these, you do unto Me?

And if we do not take up His cause, we would have to reply:

> Forgive us, O Lord, and may our hearts today heed Your call to action. We have risen from the ashes of defeat and are truly a city too busy to hate, but make us a city not too busy to love. Not too busy to reach out to all of our brothers and sisters. Not too busy to understand and accept our differences and diversity.

> Break down the barriers that divide us, because every one of us was created in Your image, O God, and You have commanded us to love one another. Help us, O God, before our differences keep us from running the race You have set before us.

> We need Your healing touch on our city and its people, O God. Where there are walls, build bridges that will connect us. Where there is fear and hatred, reveal Your love. Where there is sin in our camp, O Lord, break its hold over our lives.

> Give us leaders in our government, O God, like Nehemiah, who had vision and commitment. Leaders like Noah, who was faithful, courageous, obedient, and accountable. And we so desire the promise You made to Solomon when You told him: "Then if my people who are called by my name will humble themselves and pray and seek my face and turn from their wicked ways, I will hear from heaven and will forgive their sins and restore their land" (2 Chronicles 7:14).

O God, heal our hearts . . . heal our city . . . heal our country. Give us a fresh, new spirit with a light so bright it will be like that city set on a hill. And when we cross the finish line, I pray that You will be able to say: 'Well done, good and faithful servant.

In the holy and precious Name of Jesus, I pray. Amen.

★ ★ ★

Please . . . don't go. You can't leave yet. Not until I know you and I are going to meet again in Heaven, where Jesus has gone to prepare a new home for us.

I am thinking about all the people who are reading this book who haven't yet surrendered their lives to Christ. Have not yet said to God, "Have Your own way, Lord."

You may come to Him just as you are. Just as I came to Him on July 14, 1976. I was a mess, to say the least, but God took me and wrapped me in His arms, in His holy robes, and I have never been the same. That day I was born again—He walked into those places of sin and failure in my life, wiped the slate clean, and gave me a new beginning.

He can do the same for you.

Why don't we make it happen this moment? Your name will be instantly written in the "Lamb's Book of Life," as we read in the Book of Revelation. Then you and I will spend eternity together in Heaven, with our loved ones who have died in Christ, and there will be a great Homecoming!

It is so simple. Just pray this prayer:

"Lord Jesus, I invite You into my life. I believe You died for me and that Your death paid for my sins and provides me with the gift of eternal life. By faith, I receive that gift and acknowledge You as my Lord and Savior. Amen."

If you prayed this prayer, know that in His hands, you are safe and secure—today, tomorrow, and for all eternity. His Word says, "For I know the plans I have for you—plans for good and not for evil, to give you a future and a hope. In those days when you pray, I will listen" (Jeremiah 29:11, TLB).

Now share with someone—a Christian friend or pastor—your decision to accept Jesus as your Savior. And may God's blessing be upon you as you live the rest of your life and forever after sheltered *beneath His wings.*

My Deepest Appreciation . . .

*T*HIS BOOK IS MORE than the profile of one life or the journey of a single soul. It is the distilled essence—the fragrant aroma—of all I have gleaned from others who traveled this road before me, suffered so I could learn, and blazed the trail that carries me to a holy destination—the mansion prepared for me in my Father's House. They are pastors, poets, authors, musicians, songwriters, business associates, and dear friends. Some of these extraordinary people I have not yet had the pleasure of meeting in person, and so I thank them in absentia.

With their permission, I have included some of the powerful stories and testimonies that have profoundly impacted my story. My gratitude to God first and to the many precious people who have helped to shape my destiny.

I want to thank my co-author, Anne Severance, for her unbelievable gift of writing. From the moment our hearts connected, it was as if we had known each other forever. I will always be grateful for her patience, her gift of prayer, and her sweet spirit. And to my friend, Ann Platz, thank you for introducing us! A very special thank you to Lori Smith and Paulette Stewart, for endless hours of copying the manuscript and preparing the database to market the message of this book.

My sister, Jackie, for loving me, always wanting the best for me, and for praying for me at all times.

My brother, Sandy, for being the sweetest brother any girl could have and for believing in me in the hardest of times.

My three best friends—Glyn Weakley Teague, who is always there for me; Nancy See, my sister in Christ, prayer partner, and one who loves me unconditionally; and Ann Blackistone, who knows the worst about me, but thinks the best of me. To these three, I am forever grateful for your love and friendship.

To my high school friends, who will always be remembered because of their acceptance and ready smiles--Wyn Morris Engle, Jerry and Jim Bowden, Pat Cole McCleskey, and Elaine Tarleton Beacham—thank you for including me.

To the Founding Members of Jenny Pruitt & Associates, thank you for packing your business bags twice to follow me from Northside Realty to Buckhead Brokers and then to found Jenny Pruitt & Associates. You will always have a special place in my heart.

To the Founding Partners who came from far and near to help us launch Atlanta Fine Homes Sotheby's International Realty, thank you for your encouragement.

We went through a lot together in the beginning, and I will never forget the faith you had in David and me.

To my faithful housekeeper of thirty-seven years, Alice Kilpatrick, I can't imagine life on Mondays without you!

To two outstanding leaders, Jimmy Blanchard and Frank Skinner, you never know who is watching and desiring to emulate you. Thank you for influencing me to embrace servant leadership.

To John Barnes who introduced me to Shih-Tzus, I love my Molly and Murphy and will always remember that enjoying these adorable pets began with you.

To Max Lucado and Marie Chapian, two authors I quote often in this book, your writing has forever changed my life!

To the pastors who have had a profound influence on me and my loved ones, I thank you from the bottom of my heart. Charles Stanley, Bryant Wright, David Cooper, and Andy Stanley, your teaching has brought me into a closer walk with God.

To those who have reached their heavenly home before me, I want to thank Skipper Morrison and J.B. Denny for leading me down the path of integrity and teaching me about the real estate business. And Kim King, for believing in me when I wasn't confident about owning my own business and for being an incredible partner, thank you. You are missed by so many!

And last, but far from least, sincere appreciation to Melissa Payne Baker, for inspiring and tutoring me in the art of painting angels! Through you, they adorn my walls and my heart.

Endnotes

Chapter 1

1. Marie Chapian. *God's Heart for You* (Minneapolis, Minnesota: Bethany House, 2005), 33.

2. This guide to praying effectively has floated around for years, so I don't know who should receive the credit. But this little "formula" is a good launching pad for prayer. Try it, and the Lord will meet you exactly where you are.

3. Donald J. Wyrtzen, L.E, Singer. "Finally Home" copyright © 1971 New Spring Publishing Inc. (ASCAP) (adm. at CapitolCMGPublishing.com) / Unknown Publisher © All rights reserved. Used by permission.

4. Chapian, 106-107.

Chapter 2

1. Marie Armenia, "The Crayon Effect," *HomeLife* (May 2015), 72.

2. Chapian, 105.

Chapter 3

1. Max Lucado. *Grace Happens Here* (Nashville, TN: Thomas Nelson, 2012), 88-89.

2. Chapian, 219-220.

Chapter 4

1. Anonymous.

2. Lucado, *Grace Happens Here*, 120-121.

3. *ezer*—The Hebrew word for "helper." gotquestions.org/woman-helper-suitable.html

4. *tsela*—"Only in one verse (Genesis 2:21-22) is this Hebrew word translated 'rib.' The other 41 times, it is translated 'side, chamber, flesh.' The woman was taken from the same material from which Adam was formed." See www.godswordtowomen.org/genesis1_2.htm

5. R.E.S.P.E.C.T.—is one of those acrostics I have read or heard many times in various settings, so I don't know where it originated. As Bob and I have attempted to practice these precepts, I've added my insights on maintaining a healthy and enduring marriage.

6. For interesting reading on marriage, see John Gray, Ph.D. *Men Are from Mars, Women Are from Venus* (New York: Quill, an imprint of HarperCollins Publishers, 1992, 2004).

7. Stormie Omartian. *The Power of a Praying Parent* (Eugene, Oregon: Harvest House, 1995, 2005, 2014), 20-21. I heartily recommend this book!

8. Chapian, 32.

Chapter 5

1. Chapian, 64-65.

Chapter 6

1. Tom Barry, "Pruitt: Charity Begins at Home," *Atlanta Business Chronicle* (Oct. 3-9, 2003), 4.

2. John Maxwell. *Leadership Promises for Your Work Week* (Nashville: J

Countryman, a division of Thomas Nelson, Inc., 2006), 48. Adapted from *The Maxwell Leadership Bible*.

3. Viktor Frankl. *Man's Search for Meaning* (New York: Washington Square Press Publications of Pocket Books, 1959, 1962, 1984).

4. Learn more about Camille Kesler and the Atlanta Junior League at http://www.jlatlanta.org/ama/orig/Press_Releases_/2012-2013_President_and_BOD_Impacting_Atlanta_for_96_Years.pdf

5. The concept of this alphabetical listing is not original. I borrowed it from someone long ago. But there have been so many tweaks and alterations through the years, I have made it my own. Apologies to whomever thought of it in the first place!

6. Chapian, 87-88.

7. Chapian, 88.

Chapter 7

1. Max Lucado. *God Will Carry You Through* (Nashville: J Countryman, a division of Thomas Nelson Inc., 2013), 30-32.

2. Chapian, 93-94.

Chapter 8

1. Wage Pitt's story is told in Bob Gass. *The Word for You Today* (Alpharetta, GA: © Celebration Enterprises, 2015). Used by permission.

2. Michelle Boudin, "Heroes Among Us: Grandmother Saves Man from Fiery Car Wreck." http://www.people.com/article/grandma-pulls-disabled-man-fiery-car-wreck/

3. For more information about Atlanta Mission, click on www.atlantamission.org.

4. Read the fascinating facts about Franklin Graham's global

humanitarian organization, Samaritan's Purse, at www.samaritanspurse.org/

5. Mary Frances Bowley. *The White Umbrella* (Chicago: Moody Publishers, 2012), 15.

6. Ibid., 16.

7. Chapian, 156-157.

Chapter 9

1. http://www.franchisehelp.com/franchises/sothebys-international-realty/

2. Headline of article appearing in *Atlanta Business Chronicle,* May 15, 2007 http://www/bizjournals.com/atlanta/stories/2007/05/14/daily18.html

3. The Valley of Elah is described in goisrael.com/tourism_eng/tourist information/discover Israel/geographical regions/Pages/valley of elah.aspx

4. Herbert Lockyer, Gen. Ed. *Nelson's Illustrated Bible Dictionary* (Nashville, TN: Thomas Nelson Publishers, 1986), 437.

5. Chapian, 98-99.

Chapter 10

1. Bob Gass. *The Word for You Today* (Alpharetta, GA: © Celebration Enterprises, 2015). Used by permission.

2. Gordon Leidner, "Lincoln's Honesty," The *Washington Times* (February 20, 1999), Civil War Page. © New World Communications, Inc.

3. George Washington's father, as quoted in *George Washington's Sacred Fire* by Peter Lillback with Jerry Newcombe. (Bryn Mawr: Pennsylvania: Providence Forum Press, 2006), 693.

4. For Charles Stanley's full message on testing and trials, see www. intouch.org/wach/.../wisdom-for-life-s-trials.video.

5. Lucado, *Grace Happens Here*, 30-32.

6. Phil Cooke. *Jolt!* (Nashville: Thomas Nelson Publishers, 2011), 166-167.

7. Chapian, 75-76.

Chapter 11

1. Bob Gass. *The Word for You Today* (Alpharetta, GA: © Celebration Enterprises, 2015). Used by permission.2. Chapian, 250-251.

Chapter 12

1. Beth Moore. *Children of the Day* (Nashville: LifeWay Press, 2014), 17.

2. Note on "Family," *TouchPoint Bible*, an edition of the *Holy Bible*, New Living Translation (Carol Stream, IL: Tyndale House Publishers, Inc., 1996 by V. Gilbert Beers and Ronald A. Beers), 523.

3. Lucado, *God Will Carry You Through*, 51.

4. Chapian, 67.